EDWARD P. HAHNENBERG

A Concise Guide
To The
Documents
of
Vatican II

ST. ANTHONY MESSENGER PRESS
Cincinnati, Ohio

RESCRIPT

In accord with the Code of Canon Law, I hereby grant my permission to publish *A Concise Guide to the Documents of Vatican II* by Edward P. Hahnenberg.

Most Reverend Carl K. Moeddel
Vicar General and Auxiliary Bishop
of the Archdiocese of Cincinnati
Cincinnati, Ohio
January 22, 2007

The Permission to Publish is a declaration that a book or pamphlet is considered to be free from doctrinal or moral error. It is not implied that those who have granted the Permission to Publish agree with the contents, opinions or statements expressed.

Excerpts from *Vatican Council II: The Basic Sixteen Documents,* copyright ©1996, Rev. Austin Flannery, O.P., used with permission of the Costello Publishing Company. Scripture passages have been taken from the *New Revised Standard Version Bible,* copyright ©1989 by the Division of Christian Education of the National Council of the Churches of Christ in the U.S.A., and used by permission. All rights reserved.

Cover design by Mike Winegardner
Cover image by www.AgnusImages.com
Book design by Mark Sullivan

LIBRARY OF CONGRESS CATALOGING-IN-PUBLICATION DATA

Hahnenberg, Edward P.
A concise guide to the documents of Vatican II / Edward P. Hahnenberg.
p. cm.
Includes bibliographical references and index.
ISBN 978-0-86716-552-4 (pbk. : alk. paper) 1. Vatican Council (2nd : 1962-1965) 2. Catholic Church—Doctrines. I. Title.

BX8301962 .H285 2007
262'.52—dc22

2006037817

ISBN 978-0-86716-552-4

Published by St. Anthony Messenger Press
28 W. Liberty Street
Cincinnati, OH 45202
www.AmericanCatholic.org

Printed in the United States of America.

Printed on acid-free paper.

07 08 09 10 5 4 3 2 1

A CONCISE GUIDE TO THE DOCUMENTS OF VATICAN II

CONTENTS

....

....

Abbreviations

Citing Documents: Each of the documents of Vatican II has both an
official title and a short title. The short title is based on the first two
Latin words of the document itself. For example, the Dogmatic
Constitution on Divine Revelation is also known as *Dei Verbum* for its
opening line: "Hearing the word of God *(Dei Verbum)* reverently and
proclaiming it confidently...." In referring to individual documents, I
use the following abbreviations based on these short titles.

Citing Specific Passages: The Vatican II documents are divided into
numbered sections, called articles, which range in length from a
sentence to several paragraphs. Unless otherwise indicated, I cite
specific passages by the article number. Thus "*DV,* 12" refers to article
number 12 of the Dogmatic Constitution on Divine Revelation *(Dei
Verbum).*

AA   *Apostolicam Actuositatem*
      (ah-poh-STA-lee-kahm ahk-*too*-ah-see-TAH-tem)
      Decree on the Apostolate of Lay People

AG   *Ad Gentes* (ahd JEN-tez)
      Decree on the Church's Missionary Activity

CD   *Christus Dominus* (KREES-toos DOH-mee-nuhs)
      Decree on the Pastoral Office of Bishops in the Church

DH   *Dignitatis Humanae* (deen-yee-TAH-tees hoo-MAH-nay)
      Declaration on Religious Liberty

DV   *Dei Verbum* (DAY-ee VAIR-boom)
Dogmatic Constitution on Divine Revelation

GE   *Gravissimum Educationis*
(grah-VEE-see-m*oo*m ed-j*oo*-kah-tsee-OH-nees)
Declaration on Christian Education

GS   *Gaudium et Spes* (GOW-dee-*oo*m et spez)
Pastoral Constitution on the Church in the Modern World

IM   *Inter Mirifica* (IN-tair meer-EE-fee-kah)
Decree on the Mass Media

LG   *Lumen Gentium* (loo-men jen-tzee-*oo*m)
Dogmatic Constitution on the Church

NA   *Nostra Aetate* (NOHS-trah ay-TAH-tay)
Declaration on the Relation of the Church to Non-Christian Religions

OE   *Orientalium Ecclesiarum*
(oh-ree-en-TAHL-ee-*oo*m ek-klay-zee-AH-r*oo*m)
Decree on the Catholic Eastern Churches

OT   *Optatam Totius* (ahp-TAH-tahm toh-TSEE-uhs)
Decree on the Training of Priests

PC   *Perfectae Caritatis* (pair-FEK-tay cah-ree-TAH-tis)
Decree on the Up-to-Date Renewal of Religious Life

PO   *Presbyterorum Ordinis*
(pres-bee-TAIR-aw-r*oo*m AWR-dee-nees)
Decree on the Ministry and Life of Priests

SC   *Sacrosanctum Concilium*
(sah-kroh-SAHNK-t*oo*m kahn-CHEE-lee-*oo*m)
Constitution on the Sacred Liturgy

UR   *Unitatis Redintegratio*
(*oo*-nee-TAH-tis ray-din-tay-GRAH-tsee-oh)
Decree on Ecumenism

ACKNOWLEDGMENTS

....

To my parents, Marlene and Edward J. Hahnenberg, who lived through the Council and who—each in their own way—introduced me to it. Thank you, Mom and Dad, for everything.

Thanks go to Robert Krieg, who encouraged me early on to write this book, and to Richard Gaillardetz and William Madges, who read significant portions of the text and offered many helpful suggestions. Thanks also to the students in my fall 2005 "Why a Church?" course at Xavier University. They divided up the draft chapters, took out their own red pens and let me have it! Their questions and comments helped make this a much better guide. My colleagues in the department of theology at Xavier have been amazingly supportive, as has the entire staff at St. Anthony Messenger Press. Thanks especially to Lisa Biedenbach, who first saw promise in this project, and to Katie Carroll, who brought it into such fine form.

Finally, I thank three people who fill my life with so much joy: my wife, Julie, and our daughters, Kate and Meg.

INTRODUCTION

READING THE DOCUMENTS OF VATICAN II

The sixteen documents of the Second Vatican Council are the most important texts produced by the Catholic church in the past four hundred years. They shape virtually every aspect of church life today. But hardly anyone ever reads them.

It's not that these documents are hard to come by or difficult to understand. It's just that they need a proper introduction. This book is meant to be that introduction. Each of the following sixteen chapters offers (1) a brief history of one council document, (2) a section-by-section reading guide that highlights major themes and (3) a sampling of questions we might raise today. My goal is to empower you to read the documents themselves. For buried in their pages are both the wisdom of the past and the possibilities for the future—they hold the spirit of the Council. This book is an attempt to reclaim that spirit by unearthing the treasures in these texts.

WHAT WAS VATICAN II?

The Second Vatican Council was the twenty-first general, or ecumenical, council in the history of the Catholic church. During the autumn months of 1962, 1963, 1964 and 1965, over twenty-five hundred bishops, theological experts, other officials and observers from around the

1

world gathered in St. Peter's Basilica in Rome in order to debate the future of Catholicism. Their conversations changed things. By asking very basic questions—Who are we? What are we about?—the Council set the church on a path of inner renewal and outward engagement with the world.

Unlike previous councils, Vatican II was not called to combat some threat to the church, such as heresy or schism. Instead, it was called to respond positively to the challenges facing the modern world, to update those aspects of the church that could be updated and to reach out to other Christians in a spirit of reconciliation. These were the desires of Pope John XXIII, the inspiration and driving force behind Vatican II.

Only three months after he became pope, John XXIII announced his plans for a new ecumenical council. Such a radical idea did not go over well for some church leaders at the time. Mired in tradition, they could not imagine the church changing. For them, it was already perfect. The seventeen stunned cardinals who first heard the news responded, according to Pope John's own recollection, with "devout and impressive silence." Later, many of them voiced their concerns and objections.

But the aging pope continued to speak of the upcoming council as a means of spiritual renewal, a "new Pentecost" that would reinvigorate the church for its mission in the world. In his memorable opening speech of the council, John XXIII publicly disagreed with those "prophets of gloom" around him who saw in modern times only "prevarication and ruin." Instead, the pope believed, God is moving humanity to a new order of human relations. The church needed *aggiornamento*—"updating"—not because the church felt threatened, but because of its great desire to share Christ with all people. He pointed forward with hope: "The council now beginning rises in the Church like daybreak, a forerunner of most splendid light. It is now only dawn."

THE COUNCIL AND ITS DOCUMENTS

Pope John's vision inspired the event that was Vatican II. But the work of the Council revolved around drafting, debating, amending and approving texts.

Two days after Pope John's opening speech, the council participants settled in to begin this work. The bishops had before them several draft documents intended for discussion by the assembly. These documents were a few of the more than seventy working papers drafted by various preparatory commissions in the months leading up to the council. Because these preparatory commissions were dominated by members of the Vatican bureaucracy (called the "curia"), the drafts underlined the status quo. Their style was like that of the seminary textbooks used in Rome—philosophical, abstract, heavily reliant on past papal pronouncements and defensive toward other views. They reflected little of the biblical, liturgical and theological revivals going on in Europe at the time. Even before the Council began, a few leading bishops and cardinals from outside the curia complained that these draft documents completely failed to engage the modern world or to reach out to other Christians. They felt a new direction was needed.

At that first working session, the assembly was supposed to vote on who would fill positions on the various council committees. A list of those who had served on the preparatory commissions was distributed, with the clear expectation that these Vatican insiders would simply be reelected to lead the council commissions as well. Such a move would have seriously compromised the Council's ability to move in new directions. The Vatican insiders wanted to see the prepared drafts approved and the Council concluded as quickly as possible, with little or no change to the status quo.

Aware of this danger, Cardinal Achille Liénart of Lille, France, rose to motion that the election be postponed. He wanted bishops to have the chance to gather in regional groupings in order to draw up their own list of candidates. Cardinal Josef Frings of Cologne seconded the motion. The proposal met with such applause from the assembly that the moderators didn't know what to do. There was nothing else on the agenda. And so, the first meeting of the Second Vatican Council was adjourned after only fifteen minutes! This dramatic move, coming on the heels of the pope's speech, helped launch Vatican II on its journey of renewal. With broader representation on the Council commissions, almost all of the prepared drafts were either outright rejected, completely rewritten or substantially revised. In the end, sixteen documents were produced that reflected a new vision for the church in the modern world.

HOW TO READ THE DOCUMENTS

How are these documents to be read today? What guides our interpretation of them? The following seven principles are good to keep in mind:

1. *Pay attention to style.* Vatican II chose to leave behind the terse and legalistic language of previous councils. Instead, it employed a style meant to be invitational and persuasive. The documents favor the boundless images of Scripture over the concise definitions of philosophy. They read more like a homily than a textbook, and like a good homily, the documents seek to motivate and inspire readers to both spiritual and intellectual conversion.

2. *Be as inclusive as the Council.* In an effort to achieve as great a consensus as possible, the bishops at Vatican II frequently chose to include competing points of view rather than exclude one side or the other. Some commentators have complained that Vatican II produced "committee documents" full of compromises and internal tensions. But what is remarkable is that the bishops agreed almost unanimously on these tensions! Every document passed with overwhelming majorities— more than half passed with fewer than ten dissenting votes. Thus the Council was comfortable allowing a diversity of voices to speak.

3. *Recognize the trajectory of the Council.* The fact that various points of view are present in the council documents does not mean that all statements made were equally important to the council participants. A faithful interpretation of the documents demands that we do our best to get at the intentions of those who wrote them. What were they trying to say? What did their deliberations cause the bishops to add to a text? What did they delete? What issues were left open? Addressing such questions allows us to see that the thinking of the bishops evolved over the Council's four years. Certain themes and concepts consistently gained in importance while other themes and concepts diminished. Thus beneath the many voices allowed to speak in the final texts, we detect a movement—a trajectory toward engagement with the world, openness to other Christians, affirmation of baptismal equality and appreciation for other religions.

4. *Give special attention to the four constitutions.* The sixteen documents of Vatican II are divided into four constitutions, nine decrees and three declarations. The *constitutions* treat substantive doctrinal issues that pertain to the very nature of the church. *Decrees* and *declarations* take up more practical questions or specific areas of pastoral concern. As we will see, the decrees and declarations often presuppose the teaching found in the constitutions. Thus the constitutions (on liturgy, revelation, the church and the church in the modern world) provide the key to interpreting these other documents and the key to the Council as a whole.

5. *Avoid overemphasizing either continuity or change.* Two words have come to symbolize the twofold movement of the Council: *aggiornamento* and *ressourcement. Aggiornamento* (the Italian word for "updating") was adopted by John XXIII to describe his vision of church renewal. He wanted the church brought up-to-date in order to meet the new challenges of the modern world. *Ressourcement* (French for "return to the sources") had come to describe the work of historical

··

Where to Get the Documents

All of the council texts are available at the Vatican's official Web site (www.vatican.va; follow the "Resource Library" link). The best one-volume collection in print is *Vatican Council II: The Basic Sixteen Documents*, edited by Austin Flannery, O.P. (Costello, 1996), from which the excerpts in this book are taken. An early, but still widely used, translation can be found for purchase online and in used book stores: *The Documents of Vatican II*, edited by Walter M. Abbott, S.J. (Guild, 1966).

··

theologians who were studying Scripture, early liturgies and the great theologians of the past in the decades leading up to Vatican II. What Vatican II discovered was how well these two movements go together. The best way for the church to engage the problems of the present is to return to the rich resources of its tradition. The most radical response is to recover our roots. The change that came with Vatican II was not a major rupture from the great Christian tradition, but it was a significant shift in the church's sense of itself and its mission in the world.

6. *Keep the spirit and the letter of the Council together.* This principle underlines the thesis of this book: The best way to catch the spirit of Vatican II is to read the documents themselves.

7. *Reflect on how the Council has been received.* We cannot avoid bringing to these texts our own questions, our own experiences of Christ and community, our own sense of what Vatican II has meant for the church and the world. How these documents have been received by the whole church—the people of God—has shaped what they mean for us today. And they only take on life in dialogue with our contemporary situation.

How to Read This Book

This book is meant to serve as textbook, reading guide and reference work. It can be used in personal study, parish programs and classrooms. Each chapter begins with a brief history of one document. When taken together, these background sections tell the story of how the Council unfolded. But you need not read this book straight through (even though I think you would enjoy the experience). Any chapter can be read apart from the others. But no chapter should be read apart from the council document it treats. To do so would defeat my purpose in writing the book. To help you read the texts themselves, each chapter contains a "Reading Guide," which outlines the document, highlights central themes and explains important passages whose significance might otherwise be missed.

Each chapter ends by raising several contemporary issues connected to the document. These issues may spark individual reflection, but the questions really become interesting in the context of group discussion. I encourage you to talk about them with others. One of the wonderful things about the Second Vatican Council was the example it provided of dialogue within the church on difficult issues. Those who were paying attention at the time saw something remarkable: The church was talking about things! It seems to me we haven't done enough of this in recent years. To be a Vatican II church means more than applying the Council's teaching; it means imitating its example. If I hold out one small hope for this book, it is that it might remind the church today of this example—and get us all talking about things again.

IMPORTANT DATES

October 28, 1958	Angelo Roncalli is elected Pope John XXIII.
January 25, 1959	Pope John XXIII announces his intention to call the council.
October 11, 1962	The Second Vatican Council formally begins.
October 11–December 8, 1962	First Session of Vatican II
June 3, 1963	Pope John XXIII dies
June 21, 1963	Giovanni Battista Montini is elected Pope Paul VI.
September 29–December 4, 1963	Second Session of Vatican II
September 14–November 21, 1964	Third Session of Vatican II
September 14–December 8, 1965	Fourth Session of Vatican II
December 8, 1965	The Second Vatican Council formally closes.

THE COUNCIL'S FOUR SESSIONS

	First Session 1962	Second Session 1963	Third Session 1964	Fourth Session 1965
Topics Debated **Italics indicate significant or lengthy debates.**	• *Liturgy* • *Revelation* • Social Communication • Ecumenism • *The Church*	• *The Church* • Bishops • *Ecumenism*	• The Church • Bishops • *Religious Liberty* • *Non-Christian Religions* • Revelation • *The Lay Apostolate* • Priests • Catholic Eastern Churches • *Church in Modern World* • Missions • Religious Life • Priestly Formation • Christian Education	• *Religious Liberty* • *Church in Modern World* • Missions • Priests
Documents Issued		• Liturgy *(SC)* • Social Communication *(IM)*	• The Church *(LG)* • Catholic Eastern Churches *(OE)* • Ecumenism *(UR)*	• Bishops *(CD)* • Religious Life *(PC)* • Priestly Formation *(OT)* • Christian Education *(GE)* • Non-Christian Religions *(NA)* • Revelation *(DV)* • Lay Apostolate *(AA)* • Religious Liberty *(DH)* • Missions *(AG)* • Church in Modern World *(GS)* • Priests *(PO)*

PART ONE

....

THE FOUR CONSTITUTIONS

1

....

CONSTITUTION ON THE SACRED LITURGY

Sacrosanctum Concilium

Liturgy was the first topic debated at Vatican II, and the Constitution on the Sacred Liturgy *(SC)* was the first document issued. The bishops decided to take up liturgy first because, of all the draft documents prepared in advance for the Council, the one on the liturgy was in the best shape. This was due to the fact that the ideas in this document had been circulating for decades prior to the Council. Despite all its newness, the Second Vatican Council did not fall out of the sky. Rather it was the result of a renewal already at work.

LITURGICAL RENEWAL PRIOR TO VATICAN II

The average Catholic's experience of the Mass prior to Vatican II was of a sacred ritual that was at the same time mysterious and mechanical. Prayers were in Latin. And for much of the Mass, the priest had his back to the congregation. This tended to separate the laity from what was going on at the altar. (Except for angelic-looking altar boys dressed like priests, the laity did not enter the sacred space beyond the communion rail.) Before the Council the faithful took part in an array of devotions outside of the liturgy—ranging from benedictions and holy hours to novenas and the rosary. But at Mass they were largely passive, watching a ritual done *for* them but not *by* them.

Constitution on the Sacred Liturgy

And yet, during these years, a liturgical renewal was already at work. It began among European monks seeking ways to enrich their common prayer. And it gradually spread from monasteries to parishes. It even influenced papal teaching. Saint Pius X (1903–1914) sensed the separation many Catholics felt from the Eucharist and encouraged more frequent reception of Communion. To help, he lowered the age for First Communion. Thirty years later, Pope Pius XII (1939–1958) made the liturgy the topic of an entire encyclical letter called *Mediator Dei* ("Mediator of God"). In it, Pius XII confirmed the basic direction of the liturgical movement. He called all Catholics to full, active participation in the liturgy and said that all of the faithful constitute a holy priesthood. He recognized that Christ is present not only under the appearance of bread and wine, but also is present in the priest and the people. In terms of practice, the pope relaxed the eucharistic fast to encourage people to take Communion. And, in the early 1950s, he reformed the liturgical rites for the Easter Vigil and Holy Week.

Alongside such official support, priests and bishops tentatively began to experiment with ways to encourage lay participation. Limited use of the vernacular emerged. Missals with English translations of the Mass were promoted in the United States. And "dialogue Masses," where the whole congregation responded to the prayers of the priest, became more common. These developments—a century in the making—reached their culmination in Vatican II's Constitution on the Sacred Liturgy.

THE DEBATE AT VATICAN II

After the dramatic opening days of the Second Vatican Council, debate on the liturgy began on Monday, October 22, 1962. The debate—which ran for fifteen meetings (days, or "General Congregations")—would occupy nearly half of the Council's first session. What stands out, particularly in comparison with other documents, is how little the text changed over the course of these

> 66 It is very much the wish of the church that all the faithful should be led to take that full, conscious, and active part in liturgical celebrations which is demanded by the very nature of the liturgy, and to which the Christian people, 'a chosen race, a royal priesthood, a holy nation, a redeemed people' (1 Pet 2:9, 4-5) have a right and to which they are bound by reason of their Baptism 99 (SC, 14).

debates. The final text of SC remained substantially the same as the initial draft presented to the council assembly.

This initial draft was put together by the Preparatory Liturgical Commission during the two years leading up to the Council. The commission secretary, Father Annibale Bugnini, was a strong proponent of the liturgical movement. He helped the commission produce a document that underscored the need for reform of the liturgy and that laid out principles to guide this reform.

During the fifteen days of debate on the liturgy, 328 speeches were given by the council participants (another 297 comments were submitted in writing). The speeches ranged from enthusiastic endorsement to firm resistance. The topics that generated the most intense debate were (1) the use of the vernacular in the liturgy, (2) whether priests should be allowed to concelebrate Mass, (3) if the laity should be allowed to receive consecrated wine along with the bread and (4) what the role of bishops' conferences should be in allowing for local adaptation. Discussion on these topics revealed a split among the bishops between a majority open to reform and a minority opposed to change.

At first it was unclear how large the minority was. But a dramatic moment occurred on the seventh day of debate (October 30). On that day Cardinal Alfredo Ottaviani gave a speech strongly criticizing the document. Cardinal Ottaviani was the head of the Holy Office (now the Congregation for the Doctrine of the Faith) and the unofficial leader of those at the Council opposed to reform. He attacked the document for proposing changes that would confuse and scandalize the faithful. He asked if the council fathers were planning to launch a revolution. He had so many complaints about the text that his speech ran over the alloted time. When he was asked to stop, he refused, and his microphone was shut off. The resounding applause that followed was a clear sign that most bishops did not agree with the tone of his remarks. Perhaps resistance to the document was not as widespread as some of the speeches indicated. Two weeks later, when the first vote was taken to determine if the text was generally acceptable as a basis for further revision, only forty-six participants voted against it (out of 2,215 votes cast).

THE PACE OF THE COUNCIL

Many bishops complained about the slow pace of the debate on the liturgy. Nearly a month had passed since the start of the Council and they hadn't finished discussing the first document. Part of the problem was that the council rules were ambiguous about how long debate on a particular topic should go on. As speeches became repetitive, the bishops became bored. They left their seats to smoke or get coffee. Finally, Pope John XXIII intervened. On November 6 he gave the council presidents authority to close debate if they felt a topic had been exhausted.

The pope's announcement was made at 10:00 AM, and the debate on chapter two of the liturgy draft was terminated immediately! From that point on the Council was able to move more quickly. But by then it had already become clear to everyone that the Second Vatican

Council would need to meet again. Plans were also being made to hold a second session the following fall. It was at this second session, on December 4, 1963, that the Constitution on the Sacred Liturgy was formally approved and promulgated.

READING GUIDE

The first line of *SC* states the four goals of the "sacred council" *(Sacrosanctum Concilium)* Vatican II: (1) to energize Catholics, (2) to update church institutions, (3) to encourage the unity of all Christians and (4) to reach out to the whole world. These goals were spelled out by Paul VI, who became pope after John XXIII's death, in his opening speech at the Council's second session (September 29, 1963). They remain a wonderful summary of what Vatican II was all about.

According to *SC*, in order to achieve these goals the liturgy had to be reformed and promoted. Chapter one of *SC* lays out general principles for guiding this reform. Chapters two through seven take up the specific areas to be addressed.

CHAPTER ONE: GENERAL PRINCIPLES (*SC*, 5–46)

The Nature of Liturgy (SC, 5–13)

Jesus Christ is the source of our lives, our salvation and our worship. This emphasis on Jesus Christ—so strong at the start of *SC*—runs throughout all the documents of Vatican II. *SC* states that Christ's work of redemption was achieved through the paschal mystery of his death and resurrection. This redemption touches us through liturgy, particularly baptism and Eucharist. Following the earlier encyclical of Pius XII, *SC* recognizes that Christ is present to us in many ways. Christ is present to us in a special way under the appearance of bread and wine, but he is also present in the priest who ministers the sacraments, in the word of God that is proclaimed and in the assembly of people who gather in Christ's name. While preaching often precedes worship, and while private prayer and devotions are important, it is the liturgy that is the source and summit of all the church's activity.

....

Bar Jonah and Bar-abbas

Off a side aisle in St. Peter's Basilica were coffee shops set up to accommodate the almost three thousand men gathering each day for the council sessions. Nicknamed "Bar-Jonah" (Hebrew for "son of John," a scriptural reference to Saint Peter) and "Bar-abbas," they served as a place for bishops and their advisers to discuss (or escape!) the debates going on in the council hall. Credit for the idea goes to Pope John. He was rumored to have said that if the bishops didn't have a place to smoke their cigarettes, "they will be puffing under their miters."

....

Active Participation (*SC*, 14–20)

The full, conscious and active participation of everyone at the liturgy is to be encouraged. In fact, this is the primary concern of liturgical renewal, the goal to be considered before everything else. This call for all people to actively participate runs throughout *SC* (it is repeated over a dozen times).

Principles for Reform (*SC*, 21–46)

SC calls for a general reform of the liturgy. The reform is to be truly comprehensive, affecting not just the Mass, but the church's entire liturgical system. To accomplish this, the liturgical books are to be revised "as soon as possible." *SC* lays out general principles to guide this reform, stating that the liturgy is a communal celebration and the rites should reflect this fact. All participate in this communal celebration according to their various roles. The permission granted later in *SC* (*SC,* 57) to allow priests to concelebrate Mass (allowing more than one priest to preside over the same liturgy) reflects this move away from seeing the Eucharist as a private affair.

The overriding concern is to promote the active participation of everyone in the liturgy. For this to occur, the various prayers and rites must be easily understood by the participants. Thus the liturgy should be marked by a noble simplicity. Scripture is very important and should be used more, particularly in preaching. In a crucial passage, *SC* states that, while the Latin language is to be preserved in the Latin rite, regional conferences of bishops can allow for the use of the vernacular in their churches. This article on the vernacular (*SC,* 36) is a classic example of the gentle way in which the council participants introduced change: They first acknowledged the value of the past, and then opened a door to the future. Subsequent church implementation would greatly expand *SC*'s initial opening to local languages.

> **"** Nevertheless, the liturgy is the summit toward which the activity of the church is directed; it is also the source from which all its power flows **"** (*SC,* 10).

Since the church does not wish to impose a rigid uniformity, local adaptation of the liturgy is sometimes appropriate. One of the more important theological rediscoveries of *SC* is its vision of the local church united with its bishop around the Eucharist (see *SC,* 26, 41; also *LG,* 23, 26). The question of the relationship of the local bishop to the universal church (symbolized by the bishop of Rome, the pope) would come to dominate the debate on the Constitution on the Church. But this issue first came up in the debates on the liturgy: Just how much authority could local leaders exercise in adapting the liturgy? The minority position (voiced mainly by those bishops and cardinals who worked in the Vatican) wanted all authority to rest in Rome, with the pope and the various Vatican offices of the curia. The majority position (voiced mainly by those bishops and cardinals who led various dioceses) wanted more authority at the local level. In the end *SC* affirmed the authority of local bishops' conferences to make adaptations, provided that the "substantial unity" of the liturgy is preserved. Changes that involve a "more radical adaptation" are to be referred to Rome.

CHAPTER TWO: THE EUCHARIST (*SC,* 47–58)

Chapter two begins with a rapid review of eucharistic theology. Instituted at the Last Supper, the Eucharist is a sacrifice of Christ's Body and Blood, a memorial of his death and resurrection, a sacrament of love, a sign of unity, a bond of charity and a paschal banquet. The chapter then moves to recommendations for reform. The guiding concern is to promote the active participation of all of the faithful. Therefore, the rites are to be simplified, more Scripture is to be used, homilies are recommended, and the prayer of the faithful is to be restored. Three suggestions for reform that provoked major debates at the Council are included: (1) the vernacular is allowed, (2) Communion under both bread and wine is allowed (receiving the Lord's Body consecrated *at that Mass* is also encouraged), and (3) concelebration by multiple priests is allowed. Finally, the chapter underlines the link between the liturgy of the word and the liturgy of the Eucharist.

CHAPTER THREE: OTHER SACRAMENTS AND SACRAMENTALS (*SC*, 59–82)
The concern for the intelligibility of the rites and the active participation of the people continues in *SC*'s treatment of the other sacraments. Significant proposals made in chapter three include the restoration of the catechumenate for adults (a period of formation and instruction for those who choose to be baptized into the church), the revision of the rite of confirmation so that its connection with baptism is made clearer, the recognition that the sacrament called "Extreme Unction" is more accurately named "Anointing of the Sick" and that it is not intended only for those at the point of death, and the renewal of the funeral rites so that they express more clearly the hope of the resurrection. Certain elements from local cultures, where appropriate, can be incorporated into the church's sacramental life (for example, initiation and marriage rituals).

CHAPTER FOUR: THE DIVINE OFFICE (*SC*, 83–101)
The Divine Office, or the Liturgy of the Hours, is the church's public prayer, a recitation of psalms and other scriptural passages and prayers said throughout the day. At the time of Vatican II, these regular prayers were sung in many communities of vowed religious and were required of most clerics. Thus *SC* keeps these groups in mind. But the text also encourages the laity to take up this ancient tradition. The specific sug-

gestions made are meant to help everyone who prays the Divine Office better integrate this practice with the conditions of modern life.

CHAPTER FIVE: THE LITURGICAL YEAR (*SC*, 102–111)

Over the course of a year, the church celebrates the whole story of Jesus—from his birth and life, to his death and resurrection, to his ascension into heaven and the promise of his return. The reform of the liturgical calendar is meant to bring out more clearly the profoundly Christ-centered nature of the church's seasons. Thus, while celebrating the lives of Mary and the other saints is important, these should not distract from the church's primary focus on Jesus. In response to movements outside the church, an appendix was added to *SC,* stating that the Council was not opposed to a perpetual calendar with a fixed date for Easter—provided that all Christians agreed on it.

CHAPTERS SIX AND SEVEN: MUSIC AND ART (*SC*, 112–130)

The final chapters on sacred music and sacred art generally praise the role of art and the work of artists in promoting prayer and piety. The document encourages forms of music that enable the active participation of the people. In art, it recommends noble beauty over sumptuous display. Church buildings should be designed with the liturgy in mind. The space should allow for the active participation of the faithful.

THE DOCUMENT TODAY

UNDERSTANDING AND MYSTERY

Perhaps the greatest gain to come from the reform of the liturgy inspired by *SC* is an increase in understanding. With prayers no longer in Latin, Catholics today can more easily understand what is going on at Mass. And with many of the rituals simplified, the major symbols in the sacraments stand out more clearly. If a sacrament is both *sign* and *cause* of God's grace, it is the sign aspect that has been emphasized since Vatican II: "In this renewal, both texts and rites should be ordered so as to express more clearly the holy things which they signify" (*SC,* 21).

The Language of the Council

The documents debated at Vatican II—and the debates themselves—were all in Latin. A simultaneous-translation system for the council hall was proposed before the first session, but it never materialized. Much of the behind-the-scenes work of the council commissions and the informal discussion among bishops took place in modern languages. But the official speeches in the council hall were in Latin. This posed a real barrier for those bishops who—outside of the liturgy—hadn't used Latin since their days in seminary. And during the debate on the liturgy, the irony of this arrangement was not lost on many of the participants. They heard speeches composed in elegant classical Latin that advocated more use of the vernacular at Mass. At the same time, they had to endure some speeches delivered in sloppy, elementary-level Latin that extolled the beauty and virtues of this ancient language!

But some Catholics feel that what has been lost in all of this is a sense of mystery. For these Catholics, Sunday liturgy feels more like an informal gathering of people than the solemn worship of God. Many of these Catholics have no memories of the liturgy prior to Vatican II, but they still hunger for a greater sense of the sacred in worship. They want a feeling of awe and a recognition of God's transcendence. Other Catholics respond that God is encountered precisely in other people and in the basic activities of everyday life. This is the beauty and mystery of sacraments: God comes to us in bread and wine, God works through water, words and the touch of human hands. For these Catholics, the reform of the liturgy helps us to recognize the extraordinary in the ordinary, the sacred in the assembly.

Sometimes, differences between these two viewpoints erupt in conversations about music (traditional hymns or contemporary songs?) or church architecture (Where is the tabernacle to be placed? How are the pews to be arranged?). It is far too simplistic to label these "pre–Vatican II" and "post–Vatican II" positions. For all involved are post–Vatican II people.

But they are people with different understandings of how we relate to God and how God relates to us in the liturgy.

POPULAR DEVOTIONS

SC recommends the practice of devotions outside of the liturgy. At the same time, it recognizes that these expressions of piety revolve around the liturgy, which is far superior to any of them. Thus, devotions should be encouraged so that they harmonize with the liturgical seasons and with the eucharistic liturgy itself. But for a variety of reasons— including the translation of the Mass into English, a renewed focus on the central sacramental rites and the changing social and cultural status of American Catholics—popular devotions virtually disappeared after Vatican II. But recent years have seen a revival of devotions, both traditional European practices and those brought to U.S. Catholicism from Latin America and Asia. The challenge remains to encourage this revival in a way that fosters the active participation of all in the liturgy itself, the source and summit of all the church's activity.

LOCAL LITURGY IN A UNIVERSAL CHURCH

One of the contested points that ultimately made its way into *SC* was the claim that groups of bishops (such as national or regional conferences of bishops) have a certain authority to regulate the liturgy within their territory. Following the Council, bishops' conferences translated the revised rites into local languages and customs (always conditional on subsequent Vatican approval). However, in recent years the Vatican Congregation for Divine Worship and Discipline of the Sacraments has increasingly taken issue with liturgical proposals submitted by the U.S. bishops' conference and with translations prepared by the International Commission for English in the Liturgy (ICEL, a joint project of eleven English-speaking bishops' conferences, including the U.S.). One complaint was that too broad a use was made of inclusive language. The Vatican congregation also disagreed with the way in which Latin texts were translated into English. ICEL allowed for a dynamic and flexible translation into readable English. The Vatican prefers a more literal, word-for-word translation. (For example, the common Mass response, *"Et cum spiritu tuo"* was translated by ICEL as, "And also with you." The Vatican congregation prefers, "And with your spirit.")

Critics argue that the Vatican dismissed years of hard work by the U.S. bishops—who, after all, ought to know their own language and worship customs better than officials in Rome (who may or may not be native English-speakers). Those who defend Rome argue that the translations were of poor quality and ambiguous. They argue that the Vatican is simply defending the traditional doctrines obscured by these translations. Beneath these debates lies the challenge of maintaining liturgical unity amidst great diversity.

SOCIAL JUSTICE

Many of the early pioneers of the liturgical movement were also deeply committed to issues of poverty, peace and civil rights. They saw the call to "active participation" both in the liturgy and in the world as of a piece. The American Benedictine monk Virgil Michel (1888–1938) was an outstanding example of this dual concern. Yet *SC* is mostly silent on this connection. And post-conciliar liturgical reform has often overlooked the practical implications of our common worship.

FOR REFLECTION
- Read *SC,* 7: Where do you fall on the spectrum of understanding and mystery? How would you describe the liturgy at your parish in terms of these categories? Give examples.
- Read *SC,* 13: Describe a devotional practice that you've experienced. Do you feel that it derives from and leads to the liturgy? Why or why not?
- Read *SC,* 37–40: How far should local adaptation extend? At what point does adaptation change the basic meaning of a sacrament? Can you think of an example of local diversity that you feel enhances the celebration of the liturgy?

• Read *SC,* 10: Are there aspects of the liturgy that you feel either invite reflection on or prompt action toward social justice.

2

··

DOGMATIC CONSTITUTION ON DIVINE REVELATION
Dei Verbum

On the same day that the council participants gave their general approval to the document on liturgy (November 14, 1962), they began debate on the document on revelation. The contrast between the two was striking. Whereas the draft on liturgy had offered a positive endorsement of liturgical reform, the draft on revelation—prepared by Cardinal Ottaviani's Doctrinal Commission—was negative and defensive in tone. Widespread dissatisfaction with this draft caused a crisis for the proceedings. And the week of debate that followed proved to be the turning point of the first session, and perhaps of the entire Council.

FAULTLINES EMERGE

As soon as the draft on revelation had been introduced, Cardinal Liénart of Lille, France, rose to demand that it be completely rewritten. He questioned the way the document treated Scripture and tradition as if they were two completely independent sources of information about God. "There are not and never have been two *sources* of revelation," Liénart argued. "There is only one fount of revelation—the Word of God, the good news announced by the prophets and revealed by Christ." Other speakers criticized the document for its defensive spirit, its theological jargon, its anti-ecumenical tone, and its suspicious attitude toward biblical scholars. Cardinal Augustine Bea, the forward-looking head of the Secretariat for Christian Unity, reminded everyone of Pope John XXIII's opening speech. Vatican II was meant to be a pastoral council; it was meant to reach out to other Christians and to the whole world; it was meant to revitalize the church. But the current draft did none of these things. Bea concluded that it must be redone—made shorter, more pastoral and more open.

Defenders of the document questioned the wisdom of starting from scratch. They even questioned the

authority of the council assembly to reject a prepared draft in its entirety. Behind these arguments lay a more serious concern. They were afraid that the doctrinal purity of the faith was being clouded by loose talk of adaptation and ecumenism (attempts to reconcile divided Christian churches). The fault lines first revealed in the debate on liturgy became even more pronounced. Divisions were hardened between a core group opposed to reform and a majority in favor of it, between a doctrinal defense of the past and a pastoral openness to the future. It was unclear how the Council could proceed. Those who wanted to reject the draft knew that they would simply be sending it back to a committee headed by Cardinal Ottaviani —the one responsible for it in the first place!

A DRAFT REJECTED

After a week of debate, a surprise announcement was made. The council participants were asked to vote on whether discussion should be

....

New Truth?

"Thus it is that the church does not draw its certainty about all revealed truths from the holy scriptures alone" (*DV*, 9).

One of the points debated by theologians at the time of Vatican II was whether later church tradition added genuinely new truths to the faith not found in Scripture. Those who favored the "two-source theory" argued yes: God reveals not just through the Bible but also through the church. Others argued no: Any later doctrines are simply the development of truths whose kernel is already found in Scripture. During revision of *DV*, proponents of the "two-source theory" campaigned to insert a line that stated, in effect, that the church does not draw all revealed truths from Scripture alone. But this seemed to contradict other passages in the document that spoke of the unity of Scripture and tradition. The drafting commission eventually found a compromise in the sentence above. By shifting the emphasis from new *revealed truths* to *a certainty about revealed truths*, the commission avoided contradiction and left this theologically debated issue open.

....

stopped so that the document could be sent back to committee. In effect, this would have killed the current draft and led to a complete revision. But there was confusion among the bishops over the wording of the vote: They had to vote "yes" in order to *reject* the text. This shifted the burden of responsibility. Ordinarily, a two-thirds majority was needed to *approve* a text—meaning that only one-third of the vote was needed to reject it. But now those opposed to the draft had to gather a full two-thirds. When the ballots were counted, they were just 105 votes short of the number needed to reject the text (out of a total of 2,209 votes cast). It seemed that the Council was stuck with a document that a clear majority found unacceptable.

The very next day Pope John XXIII intervened. Despite the vote, Pope John ordered that the draft be withdrawn. He decided that the document would be revised by a new mixed commission, with Cardinals Ottaviani and Bea as joint presidents. This solved the impasse. The pope's action both carried out the will of the majority and ensured that those responsible for the revisions would have to take into account the concerns of both sides.

A NEW SPIRIT, A NEW DOCUMENT

Pope John's announcement breathed a new spirit of hope into the Council. It now seemed that real renewal was possible. But work on the document on revelation had only just begun. Months of debate and redrafting by the mixed commission lay ahead. Among the many issues to be resolved, three were especially difficult: (1) the relationship of Scripture and tradition, (2) the inerrancy of the Bible and (3) the historical nature of the Gospels. These issues preoccupied the commission, they were again debated in the council hall during the third session (1964), and they were the subject of tortuous negotiations on specific word choices down to the final editing of the text. When the Dogmatic Constitution on Divine Revelation *(DV)* was formally approved and promulgated on November 18, 1965, its story had become one with the Council itself. The final text reflects the council's transformation from a dogmatic defense of "The Tradition" to a positive, pastoral embrace of God's self-revelation to the world.

BEHIND THE SCENES

The public debates in the council hall were important. But most of the work of Vatican II was done behind the scenes. For many bishops, going to Rome for the Council meant going back to school. Lectures were arranged and widely attended. These talks featured prominent theologians who literally brought the bishops up to date on recent research. National bishops' conferences organized think tanks to advise them on issues, position papers were drafted, and representatives from different groups met to strategize. After the preparatory documents were released, numerous theological critiques were published and

The Word of God at the Council

Each day of the Council, before debate began, the book of the Gospels was solemnly enthroned in a place of prominence near the altar of St. Peter's. This gesture emphasized the importance of Scripture at Vatican II, for the word of God symbolically presided over the proceedings.

alternative versions were circulated. And so when Cardinal Liénart rose to demand that the draft on revelation be rejected, he was articulating a growing consensus made possible by the behind-the-scenes movement of bishops and theologians working together.

READING GUIDE

The Prologue of *DV* makes this important point: We *hear* the word of God *(Dei Verbum)* before we proclaim it. The shift from the first draft to the final draft of *DV* was, in many ways, a shift in approach to the Bible—from using the Bible as a "proof text," quoted only to support conclusions already drawn, to seeing it as the primary witness of God's revelation.

The first three chapters of *DV* treat foundational theological issues: from the nature of revelation itself, to the way in which revelation is handed on, to the place of the Bible within this process. The last three chapters of *DV* are more descriptive.

CHAPTER ONE: REVELATION ITSELF *(DV, 2–6)*

Revelation is not just words about God, it is a living encounter with God. The first draft of this document offered what we might call a propositional view of revelation. Revelation was equated with certain propositions—statements that give us access to interesting information about God. But later revisions of the text balanced this with a more relational, personal approach to revelation. God not only reveals the divine will, God reveals God's very self. The goal of this revelation is to invite people into fellowship with God and with one another *(DV, 2)*. Jesus is the living example of this invitation. We speak of the Bible as the "Word of God." But it is better to think of the Bible as the inspired *testimony* to the living Word of God, who is Jesus (*DV,* 4). Faith then is as much the act of committing one's whole life to Christ as it is assenting to certain truths we believe (*DV,* 5).

CHAPTER TWO: THE TRANSMISSION OF DIVINE REVELATION (*DV,* 7–10)

The relationship of Scripture and tradition has been controversial since the Reformation. When the Reformers cried out, "Scripture alone!" the Catholic church replied, "Tradition too!" The church wanted to protect

❝ By this revelation, then, the invisible God (see Col 1:15, 1 Tim 1:17), from the fullness of his love, addresses men and women as his friends (see Ex 33:11; Jn 15:14–15), and lives among them (see Bar 3:38), in order to invite and receive them into his own company **❞** (DV, 2).

what it saw as legitimate historical developments in doctrine, sacramental practice and church structure against the Reformers' claim that these were unbiblical. And so, many Catholics defended later church tradition as a separate, almost independent source of revelation alongside the Bible.

This "two-source theory" made its way into the preparatory draft of *DV.* But it immediately drew fire from Cardinal Liénart and many others at the Council. They pointed out that this theory was a relatively new interpretation, with little support in the first fifteen hundred years of church teaching. They also argued that it was too simplistic, obscuring the essential truth that revelation is a cohesive whole with *one* source, God. It is this cohesive whole that is passed on in different ways, both in writing and in the practices of the church. Cardinal Liénart's objection eventually carried the day. In the end, *DV* states that Scripture and tradition "make up a single sacred deposit of the word of God" (*DV,* 10). The two flow from the same divine wellspring and move toward the same goal (*DV,* 9).

Chapter two also recognizes that the church's insight into revelation develops over time and that tradition progresses. In this process, the whole church—all of the faithful—has a role to play (*DV*, 8). The magisterium is not superior to the word of God, but is its servant (*DV*, 10).

CHAPTER THREE: THE INSPIRATION AND INTERPRETATION OF SCRIPTURE (*DV*, 11–13)

In a few short paragraphs, chapter three takes up three huge topics: the inspiration, inerrancy and interpretation of Scripture.

First, the chapter affirms the divine inspiration of Scripture, acknowledging both the work of God and the work of human beings. The authors of the Bible were not robots taking dictation from God. Instead, God made use of their human abilities, knowledge and limitations —they are "true authors."

Second, chapter three affirms the inerrancy of Scripture, even though it doesn't use the word. Many Catholics are surprised to learn that the church teaches that the Bible is inerrant. This is because they usually equate inerrancy with a particular view that holds that the Bible is completely free from error on all things, including scientific and historical facts. The first draft of the document on revelation actually promoted this view, stating that the Bible is without error on all truths "religious or profane." This claim raised a storm of protest during the council debates, perhaps none as strong as a speech at the Council's third session by Cardinal Franziskus König of Vienna (October 2, 1964). König warned that the church could not ignore the simple fact that the Bible contains many errors about historical events and scientific explanations. The Council then debated whether the document should distinguish between sacred and profane truths in the Bible—the first always without error, the second sometimes including error. But in the end *DV* avoided this distinction altogether. It affirms that the entire Bible is inspired and that all its books "firmly, faithfully and without error, teach that truth which God, for the sake of our salvation, wished to see confided to sacred scriptures" (*DV*, 11). The key phrase is "for the sake of our salvation." *DV* avoids dividing the Bible into sacred and profane truths, and says instead that it depends on one's perspective. The *whole* Bible is without error—but with an eye to salvation, not with an eye to historical or scientific accuracy.

Finally, the interpretation of Scripture is to make use of the methods of contemporary biblical scholarship. To get at what God intends to communicate in a particular passage, we must first ask what the human authors intended to communicate—for God is working precisely through these human beings. But we can only understand the author's intention if we understand something about his or her historical context and the different kinds of literary genres employed (*DV,* 12).

CHAPTER FOUR: THE OLD TESTAMENT (*DV*, 14–16)

This descriptive chapter—generally considered the weakest of the document—reflects on God's revelation in the Hebrew Bible. It notes that these Scriptures have a lasting value (*DV,* 14) and that they serve to prepare for the coming of Christ (*DV,* 15).

CHAPTER FIVE: THE NEW TESTAMENT (*DV*, 17–20)

The most contentious issue of chapter five was the question of the historical nature of the Gospels. Some bishops were disappointed with an earlier draft that stated that the Gospel authors "told the honest truth" about Jesus. They wanted the text to more clearly affirm that the Gospels reflect accurately the *historical facts* of Jesus' life. The commission responded by affirming the general historical character of the Gospels, without insisting that every last detail of Jesus' life is factually represented.

This chapter was helped by a recently published document of the Pontifical Biblical Commission, "The Historical Truth of the Gospels" (1964). This document pointed out that the four Gospels are most likely not the writings of eyewitnesses. Rather, the Gospels developed through a process that can be described in three stages: (1) the ministry of Jesus, (2) a period of oral transmission and preaching by the apostles, and (3) the actual composition of the Gospels by evangelists who drew on the oral traditions and retold the story of Jesus in light of the situations in their own churches.

CHAPTER SIX: SCRIPTURE IN THE LIFE OF THE CHURCH (*DV*, 21–26)
This chapter begins by comparing the Bible to the Eucharist, speaking of the "one table" of the word of God and the body of Christ from which we are fed (*DV*, 21). It states that everyone should have access to the Bible. And so it encourages new translations to be made, affirms the work of Scripture scholars and expects all ministers to study carefully the sacred books so that the faithful may receive instruction and nourishment from the word.

THE DOCUMENT TODAY

REVELATION AND OTHER RELIGIONS
Some theologians today ask if divine inspiration is reserved exclusively to the Christian Bible. On the one hand, *DV* makes no mention of other non-Christian religions in its treatment of revelation. It speaks only of the Old and New Testaments as inspired by God. On the other hand, it states that all people can come to know God by reflecting on the created world (*DV*, 3, 6). Other documents of Vatican II clearly affirm the possibility of salvation for non-Christians, teaching that the church rejects nothing that is true and holy in other religions, which often reflect "a ray of that truth which enlightens all men and women" (*NA*, 2; see *LG*, 16).

These statements lead some to ask: If other religions contain a "ray of truth," and if all truth comes ultimately from God, then shouldn't we acknowledge that God is at work in these religions? Aren't the sacred Scriptures of other religious traditions—such as the Qur'an of Islam or the Upanishads of Hinduism—in some sense inspired? Others would respond that this undermines the unique inspired character of the Bible.

BIBLICAL FUNDAMENTALISM
In recent years there has been an upsurge in various forms of biblical fundamentalism. These movements range from the evangelical desire

to make the Bible the standard for moral living to the rigid rejection of scientific theories or historical facts that seem to contradict the "literal truth" of the Bible. The appeal of these movements is the simplicity and security of belief in a world that often seems threatening. The risk is that they often overlook the complexity of the Scriptures themselves. One place in which fundamentalism has appeared in the news and in public policy is in the debate over teaching evolution in schools. In some states opponents of evolution have successfully promoted their views by inserting curricula that emphasize that evolution is only a theory and that offer alternative theories (such as "intelligent design") more in line with the creation stories of Genesis. For these groups evolutionary theory and the Bible are in clear conflict.

THE CRITICAL FUNCTION OF SCRIPTURE

DV presents a very positive vision of the role of the Bible in the life of the church. It describes the harmonious working together of Scripture scholars and church leaders. And it pictures the development of tradition as the seamless unfolding of truths already latent in the preaching of the apostles. But we know that the picture is not always so rosy. In fact, the biblical scholarship encouraged by *DV* has actually served to challenge some of the traditional beliefs and practices cherished by Catholics. Scholars have called into question the scriptural basis for certain simplistic assumptions about the origins of the sacraments, the ordained priesthood, the role of Peter or Mary and the place of women in the church. Furthermore, at times the Bible displays a prophetic edge, as when Jesus' attitude toward the poor and his acceptance of the sinner confront our own failings as Christians.

THE EXPERIENCE OF SUFFERING

DV repeats the traditional teaching that no new public revelation is to be expected (*DV,* 4). But it does not deny that we continue to meet God in and through our experience of the world. Some today affirm with great conviction that God is met—and is thus revealed to us—most powerfully in those who are poor, marginalized and forgotten. A whole way of doing theology—called "liberation theology"—grew up out of the experience of human suffering in Latin America. Faced with the violence of oppressive political regimes and the poverty of unjust economic structures, theologians and other Christians are claiming that God is revealed here in a profound "No!: This should not be so." Children should not starve, women should not be raped, the innocent should not be executed. In such a context, faith as a response to God's revelation can only mean action—working to overcome these injustices.

FOR REFLECTION

- Read *DV,* 3–4: Does God reveal through other religions? Are their sacred writings inspired? In explaining why or why not, describe how you understand inspiration.
- Read *DV,* 11–13: Are the theory of evolution and the Bible stories of creation in conflict? Why or why not? How would the treatment of inerrancy in *DV* respond to biblical fundamentalism?
- Read *DV,* 21: In what ways do you see the Bible challenging your own life and the life of the church? How might we respond? Describe one homily you've heard that drew on the Bible in a prophetic way. What made it powerful?
- Read *DV,* 2: Can we speak of God's self-revelation in the "negatives" of our world? Can you think of an example from your own life? How do we understand a person of faith as one who "freely commits oneself entirely to God" (*DV,* 5) in such a context?

3

....

DOGMATIC CONSTITUTION ON THE CHURCH
Lumen Gentium

The Dogmatic Constitution on the Church *(LG)* is, in many ways, the crowning achievement of the Second Vatican Council. Vatican II was a council of the church, for the church and about the church. And nowhere is the church's own self-understanding—its sense of itself, its nature and its purpose—laid out as clearly as in *LG*.

LG went through three major drafts, corresponding to the first three sessions of the Council.

THE FIRST DRAFT (1962)

For almost four hundred years Catholic thinking about the church (or "ecclesiology") was dominated by a sort of philosophical "defensive driving." When the Protestant Reformers challenged the pope, the priesthood and the sacramental structures of the church, Roman Catholics responded by vigorously defending precisely those elements that were under attack. This led to an overemphasis on these elements; therefore, the visible and structural aspects of the church—its hierarchy and its institutions—were highlighted. The spiritual and communal dimensions were often neglected.

Dogmatic Constitution on the Church

First Draft (1962)

Chapter One: The Nature of the Church Militant

Chapter Two: The Members of the Church Militant and Its Necessity for Salvation

Chapter Three: The Episcopate as the Highest Level of the Sacrament of Orders; The Priesthood

Chapter Four: Residential Bishops

Chapter Five: The States of Evangelical Perfection

Chapter Six: The Laity

Chapter Seven: The Magisterium of the Church

Chapter Eight: Authority and Obedience in the Church

Chapter Nine: The Relationship Between Church and State

Chapter Ten: The Necessity of Proclaiming the Gospel to the Nations of the World

Chapter Eleven: Ecumenism

Appendix

Second Draft (1963)

Chapter One: The Mystery of the Church

Chapter Two: The Hierarchical Constitution of the Church and the Episcopate in Particular

Chapter Three: The People of God and the Laity in Particular

Chapter Four: The Call to Holiness in the Church

Third and Final Draft (1964)

Chapter One: The Mystery of the Church

Chapter Two: The People of God

Chapter Three: The Church Is Hierarchical

Chapter Four: The Laity

Chapter Five: The Universal Call to Holiness

Chapter Six: Religious

Chapter Seven: The Pilgrim Church

Chapter Eight: Our Lady

Explanatory Note

Later, when modern science and philosophy seemed to threaten the church's entire belief system, Catholics rallied around their pope. They saw defending the institution as the best way to defend the faith. And so the First Vatican Council (1869–1870) defined papal primacy and papal infallibility—hoping to find a champion of stability and truth in a rapidly changing world. Because of Vatican I's focus, subsequent Catholic ecclesiology gave an enormous amount of attention to the pope, giving the impression that the Catholic church was practically equivalent to the papacy.

Many of the bishops at Vatican II wanted to correct this imbalance, but they were disappointed when they saw the preparatory draft on the church. In it the "defensive driving" continued. This first draft had some redeeming qualities: It called the church the mystical body of Christ; it affirmed the role of the laity; it contained an initial opening to ecumenism. But by and large the draft was marked by the defensive preoccupation with church structures that had shaped official church teaching since the Reformation. And it was roundly criticized in speeches by Cardinals Leo Josef Suenens of Belgium, Giovanni Battista Montini of Milan and others. The most powerful attack came from Bishop Emil Josef De Smedt (Belgium), who accused the draft of *triumphalism* (a pompous and romantic vision of the church that overlooks its flaws), *clericalism* (seeing the church as a pyramid with pope on top and laypeople on the bottom) and *juridicalism* (an obsession with rules and overlooking the spiritual dimension). By the end of a week of debate—the last week of the first session—it was clear that the document would have to be radically redone.

THE SECOND DRAFT (1963)

John XXIII died on June 3, 1963, and, as many expected, Cardinal Montini of Milan was elected Pope Paul VI. The new pope quickly assured everyone that he fully intended to continue Pope John's Council, and he indicated that the document on the church would be the first item of business when the bishops gathered again in the fall.

Meanwhile, the commission responsible for revising the church document decided to drop the first draft and work off of an entirely new text, composed by the Belgian theologian Gérard Philips. This second draft had a much simpler overall structure. Eleven chapters had been reduced to four: (1) the mystery of the church, (2) the hierarchy (bishops in particular), (3) the people of God (the laity in particular), and (4) the call of all to holiness. The shift in the title of the first chapter—from the "church militant" to the "church as mystery"—indicates the new draft's recovery of the spiritual dimension of the church.

Even before the second draft was sent to the bishops in the summer of 1963, a recommendation was made about the arrangement of its chapters. At a meeting of the Council's Central Commission, Cardinal Suenens suggested that the third chapter on "The People of God and the Laity in Particular" be split, and that all material on the people of God be combined to form a new chapter that would be inserted *before* the chapter on the hierarchy. The commission liked this idea and agreed to put it before the bishops in the fall, when it found wide support, and the change was eventually made to the third draft of the document. This editorial change symbolized the profound theological transformation going on. The church is not first the clergy; it is first of all the whole people of God. Believers share a oneness and a baptismal equality that precedes the distinctions among different roles in the community.

Over half of the second session of Vatican II was dedicated to debating the document on the church (more time in council debate was spent on this document than any other at Vatican II). One of the most contentious issues that emerged among these bishops working together was precisely how bishops should work together! "Collegiality" referred to the idea that the pope shares authority with his brother bishops. It was a hotly contested issue. Some argued that, according to the ancient tradition of the church, the pope and the bishops together belong to a college, which, as a whole, exercises supreme authority in the governance of the church. Others argued that collegiality was a novelty. If the pope shares authority, they claimed, his authority would be weakened. He would lose his ability to lead the universal church effectively.

During the week and a half of debate, speeches seemed evenly divided. And so, the moderators decided to hold a series of "orienting votes" to determine the mind of the Council on collegiality (and on whether the permanent diaconate should be reinstituted). After some delay the straw vote was taken on October 30. The results showed overwhelming support for the principle of collegiality (and strong support for deacons). While the minority side debated the binding nature of this straw vote, it marked a breakthrough for the Council in moving forward on the document.

> **"** It is therefore quite clear that all Christians in whatever state or walk in life are called to the fullness of Christian life and to the perfection of charity, and this holiness is conducive to a more human way of living even in society here on earth **"** (LG, 40).

Where Is the Church?

"This church, constituted and organized as a society in the present world, *subsists in* the Catholic Church, which is governed by the successor of Peter and by the bishops in communion with him. Nevertheless, many elements of sanctification and of truth are found outside its visible confines" (LG, 8, emphasis added).

The Council debated whether the true church of Christ is equivalent to the Roman Catholic church. The first draft of the church document stated that "there is only one true Church of Jesus Christ...[which Christ] entrusted to Saint Peter and his successors, the Roman pontiffs, to be governed; therefore only the Catholic Roman has a right to be called the church." This claim was toned down in a subsequent draft, which stated simply that the church of Christ "is (est) the Catholic church." But many bishops still found this objectionable, for the simple identification implied that Protestant and Orthodox churches are not churches in any real sense. Thus, in what might be the single most important word change of the whole Council, the Latin *est* was replaced with *subsistit in*. The church of Christ is not identical with the Catholic church; the church of Christ "subsists in"—it exists or lives in—the Catholic church, but not exclusively there. While fully present in the Catholic church, elements of truth and sanctification can be encountered in non-Catholic Christian communities as well. The ecumenical implications of this tentative opening are enormous.

....

THE FINAL DRAFT (1964)

At the start of the third session, the bishops had before them a completely revised draft that was divided into fifty-five smaller sections that would be voted on individually (the controversial chapter on the hierarchy was itself divided into thirty-nine separate votes). These individual sections—and the document as a whole—passed with large majorities. Part of this was due to Pope Paul VI, who went out of his way to address the concerns of the minority, often recommending minor changes that nuanced the document's treatment of controversial issues. To this end, a footnote clarifying the meaning of collegiality was inserted after the final text had been approved—a move that frustrated many of the council participants for its obvious attempt to placate the minority.

READING GUIDE

LG begins by putting the church in its place. It is *Christ* who is the light of the world *(Lumen Gentium)*. The church merely reflects this light—just as the moon reflects the light of the sun.

The eight chapters of the document can be paired thematically: Chapters one and two treat the church's divine origin and historical existence, chapters three and four treat different roles in the church, chapters five and six treat holiness and religious life, and chapters seven and eight treat the saints and Mary.

CHAPTER ONE: THE MYSTERY OF THE CHURCH (*LG*, 1–8)

The Church of the Trinity (LG, 1–4)

Article 1 calls the church a sacrament. The word *sacrament* tradition-ally referred only to the seven sacraments. These were defined as "visible signs of invisible grace," but theologians in the years leading up to Vatican II wanted to broaden the notion. If sacraments are visible signs of the invisible God, then isn't Jesus Christ himself the *first* sacra-ment? And isn't the church *as a whole* a sacrament of Christ? For the church is a visible sign of Jesus who is no longer visible to us. *LG* fol-lows this trajectory. Calling the church a sacrament has the advantage of affirming the visible structures of the church, but in a way that points us to the deeper, invisible reality of God's presence in the community.

LG then describes how the church flows out of the life of the Trinity: Father (*LG*, 2), Son (*LG*, 3) and Holy Spirit *(LG, 4)*.

Images of the Church (LG, 5–7)

The mystery of the church means that no simple definition can capture it. The best we can do is speak in metaphors and images. This is, after all, the way Jesus spoke when he tried to describe the kingdom of God. The church is not the kingdom of God. It is only "the seed and the beginning of that kingdom" (*LG*, 5). This recognition tempers the tri-umphalism of past ecclesiologies. Chapter one offers a variety of bib-lical images for the church. The church is like a sheepfold, a farm, a field, a building, God's temple, the spouse of Christ and, finally, the body of Christ.

A Visible Society and a Spiritual Community (LG, 8)

Like the visible and invisible dimension of the sacraments, the visible church and the spiritual community are not two separate things. Together they form the one church of Christ. This church of Christ "subsists in" the Catholic church, that is, it exists in its fullness there, but not exclusively. Many elements of truth and sanctification are found in other churches and Christian communities as well.

Finishing Vatican I

Vatican I's (1869–1870) definitions of papal primacy and papal infallibility were only part of its original agenda. At the time the bishops were debating a document on the church as a whole. But the outbreak of the Franco-Prussian War interrupted the Council after the bishops had completed only four of the fifteen chapters of this document—only the chapters on the papacy were promulgated. Thus, many saw Vatican II as finishing the work of Vatican I by going on to treat, not just the pope, but the other bishops and the whole community of believers.

CHAPTER TWO: THE PEOPLE OF GOD
(*LG*, 9–17)

Chapter two discusses the mystery of the church as it is lived out in history. It is thus intimately related to chapter one. In fact, the drafting commission explained that the two chapters were separated only because a single chapter would have been too long.

New Israel (LG, 9)

The theme of the church as "the people of God" had become more and more popular among Catholic theologians in the years leading up to Vatican II. It was favored over the more abstract view of the church as the mystical body of Christ (the subject of Pius XII's 1943 encyclical on the church, *Mystici Corporis*) for at least two reasons: (1) "People of God" affirms the common identity and equal dignity of everyone in the church, and (2) it captures the dynamic quality of the church as a people on a journey. Chapter two picks up these themes. It begins with God's call to the people Israel, a call extended in a new way to the followers of Christ.

The People of God and the Work of Christ (LG, 10–13)

The threefold work of Christ as priest, prophet and king illuminates the work of the whole people of God.

The biblical image of the priesthood of all believers (1 Peter 2:4–10) had been held suspect by Catholics since the Reformation. When Martin Luther proclaimed the priesthood of all believers, he seemed to be denigrating the priesthood of the ordained. But Vatican II recovered this concept. It confidently affirmed the priesthood of the faithful and carefully distinguished it from the ministerial priesthood. The two "differ essentially" (*LG,* 10). While the priesthood of the faithful (which includes *all* of the faithful—laity and clergy) consists of those spiritual sacrifices in life that go along with being a disciple of Jesus, the ministerial or hierarchical priesthood exists within and *in order to serve* this priesthood of all believers.

❝ "[God] has, however, willed to make women and men holy and to save them, not as individuals without any bond between them, but rather to make them into a people who might acknowledge him and serve him in holiness ❞ (*LG,* 9).

The whole church's prophetic witness to Christ and its unity in belief manifests a "sense of the faithful"—a term that describes the community's intuitive grasp of what is true. Formal church teaching reflects—and in fact can never contradict—the corporate faith of the church. Moreover, God's Spirit grants special charisms to individuals. These are spiritual gifts that serve the good of the church (*LG,* 12).

The people of God are spread throughout the world, diverse and oriented toward the heavenly kingdom of God.

Degrees of Communion (*LG,* 14–17)

The shift in emphasis from "body of Christ" to "people of God" allowed the Council to avoid the complicated question of who is and who is not a member of Christ's body. Instead, *LG* speaks of the various ways others are related to the people of God. The text moves outward from the Catholic faithful to catechumens (those preparing for baptism), to other Christians, to the Jewish people, to Muslims, to those of other religions, to those who do not even know God. Behind it all lies an optimism about the possibility of salvation for all people who strive to live a good life. But the recognition that people of all faiths can be saved does not make any less urgent the call to proclaim Christ and spread the gospel.

....

The Dependence of Other Documents on *Lumen Gentium*

SECTIONS OF *LUMEN GENTIUM*	DOCUMENTS DEPENDING ON THESE SECTIONS
8, 15	Decree on Ecumenism *(UR)*
13, 23	Decree on Catholic Eastern Churches *(OE)*
16	Declaration on Non-Christian Religions *(NA)*
17	Decree on Missionary Activity *(AG)*
18–27	Decree on Pastoral Office of Bishops *(CD)*
28	Decree on Ministry and Life of Priests *(PO)*
28	Decree on Training of Priests *(OT)*
30–38	Decree on the Lay Apostolate *(AA)*
43–47	Decree on Renewal of Religious Life *(PC)*

....

CHAPTER THREE: THE HIERARCHY (*LG*, 18–29)

The Nature of the Episcopate (LG, 18–24)

The most hotly debated issue in this document was the issue of collegiality (shared authority among the bishops and the pope). The majority of council participants wanted to move away from a monarchical vision in which all authority and power flowed downward from the pope. They favored greater collaboration and wanted to affirm that the pope and bishops *together* hold supreme authority in the church. But a vocal minority opposed this shift. And so the final text of chapter three is full of the qualifications, technical distinctions and repeated explanations necessary to develop consensus. Three arguments stand out that reveal the chapter's basic support of collegiality.

First, chapter three begins in a very traditional way by locating the origins of the episcopate in Jesus' decision to choose twelve apostles. But it adds that the apostles formed a college or permanent assembly headed by Peter (*LG*, 19). *LG* sees authority passing *to Peter and the apostles together.* This authority is then passed to the whole college of bishops, with the pope as its head.

Second, the text affirms the sacramentality of episcopal consecration. By this consecration bishops receive "the fullness of the sacrament of Orders" and the power to sanctify, teach and lead (*LG,* 21). Since the Middle Ages theologians were undecided about whether consecration as a bishop was a true sacrament. Many thought that becoming a bishop simply meant that the pope granted the new bishop permission and jurisdiction to lead a diocese. *LG* removed this ambiguity: Bishops receive their power not from the pope, but from the sacrament (a power which is, of course, always exercised in union with the pope and the whole college of bishops). Thus, the bishop is not the pope's "vicar" or representative, he is a sacramentally empowered collaborator in the pope's ministry of service to the whole church.

Third, *LG* emphasized the particular church (the diocese) and the role of the bishop within it. The particular church is not a branch office of an international church corporation, it is not an administrative subset of the "real" church. It *is* the church of God in a particular place. It is "wholly church, but not the whole church." Thus *LG* can say that it is in and from the particular churches, "modelled on the universal church," that "the one and unique catholic church exists" (*LG,* 23). Such a vision further supports collegiality, for each bishop represents his own church and, together with the pope, all bishops represent the whole church.

The Work of Bishops and the Work of Christ (*LG,* 25–27)
After its discussion of collegiality, chapter three discusses the tasks of the bishop according to the threefold work of Christ. The prophetic work of the bishop is exercised by preaching the gospel, which holds pride of place among all the duties of the bishop. Here, too, *LG* spells out the teaching authority of bishops. After reviewing the ordinary (non-infallible but not-unimportant) ways in which bishops and popes teach every day, article 25 describes the three ways in which something can be taught infallibly: (1) by all bishops, scattered around the world, when they are in agreement that a particular teaching is to be held

Prophet, Priest and King

Christ's threefold work as prophet, priest and king was first systematically laid out by the Protestant Reformer John Calvin. But in the nineteenth and twentieth centuries Catholics began to adopt this framework as a helpful way of describing the threefold work of the clergy to teach (prophet), sanctify (priest), and lead (king). Vatican II expanded it broadly to include all aspects of the church's ministry of word, worship and service. And it became a major organizing principle in the council documents. It structures the discussion of the whole people of God (LG, 10–13), bishops (LG, 24–27; CD, 12–16), priests (CD, 30; PO, 4–6) and laity (LG, 34–36; AA, 2).

definitively (this category, called the "ordinary universal magisterium" is notoriously difficult to pin down; LG identifies no mechanism for determining when all bishops are in agreement); (2) by all bishops, gathered in an ecumenical council, when defining a matter of faith or morals; and (3) by the pope, when he speaks as head of the church, on a matter of faith or morals, with the clear intention of binding the church. The priestly work of the bishop is seen most clearly in his oversight of the liturgical life of his diocese. And the bishop's kingly work is found in servant leadership, in imitation of Christ the good shepherd.

Priests (LG, 28)

Only one article in the whole of LG is dedicated to priests, a fact that raised many complaints from the bishops at Vatican II. The separate Decree on the Ministry and Life of Priests (PO) spells out in greater detail the themes summarized here: that the priest shares in the priesthood of Christ and serves as an important collaborator with the bishop in shepherding the people of God.

Deacons (LG, 29)

This article restores the ancient practice of the diaconate as a permanent order in the church and opens it up to married men. It recognizes a wide range of ministries proper to deacons, claiming that they are ordained "not for the priesthood, but for the ministry." This short, confident article hides both the strong resistance of some bishops to the idea of married deacons, on the one hand, and the passionate pleas of many bishops from missionary areas who spoke of the pastoral need, on the other.

CHAPTER FOUR: THE LAITY (*LG*, 30–38)

The chapter on the laity changed the least from the first preparatory draft to the final text of *LG*. Chapter four locates the laity within the context of the whole people of God and describes them as those members of the faithful who are not in holy orders or religious life. They are, by baptism, incorporated into Christ, made to share in his priestly, prophetic and kingly work (see *LG,* 34–36), and empowered to play an active part in the mission of the church.

In striving to articulate the distinctive contribution of the laity, *LG* highlights the laity's secular characteristic: "It is the special vocation of the laity to seek the kingdom of God by engaging in temporal affairs and directing them according to God's will" (*LG,* 31). But this emphasis was not meant to create a rigid division between laity in the world and clergy in the church. In fact, when this text was presented to the bishops at the Council for a vote, Bishop John Wright of Pittsburgh explained that the drafting commission did not intend to provide an "ontological definition" of the layperson, only a "typological description." That is, they weren't seeking to define the very essence (ontology) of what it means to be lay; they were simply observing that laypeople "typically" work in the world, raise families, hold secular jobs and so on. Indeed, the document recognizes that clergy sometimes hold secular occupations. And it acknowledges a variety of ways laypeople serve within the church.

CHAPTER FIVE: THE UNIVERSAL CALL TO HOLINESS (*LG*, 39–42)

Chapters five and six of *LG* began as a single chapter on the "States of Evangelical Perfection," which treated only consecrated religious life (those who take vows of poverty, chastity and obedience—such as sisters, nuns, brothers, monks and religious order priests). For the second draft of the church document, this chapter was entirely rewritten, with a new focus on the call of *the whole church* to holiness. But many bishops and religious superiors at the Council felt religious life was in danger of getting lost in this arrangement. They wanted religious to have a chapter of their own. So a compromise was reached in the final document. Chapter five would treat holiness in general, and chapter six would treat holiness in religious life.

Chapter five begins by stating that the church is blessed by Christ. Thus everyone in it is called to be holy. Priests and nuns no longer hold a monopoly on sanctity. Instead, the chapter describes the call to holiness of a variety of groups: bishops, priests, other ministers, married couples, parents, widows, single people and those who suffer. Love is the way we respond to this call.

CHAPTER SIX: RELIGIOUS (*LG*, 43–47)
Since the early church the evangelical counsels (poverty, chastity and obedience) have held a special place in Christian attempts to live a life of holiness. Members of religious orders embrace these ideals in a public and permanent way. They are a sign to the world, a witness that inspires the whole church to holiness (*LG*, 44).

CHAPTER SEVEN: THE PILGRIM CHURCH (*LG*, 48–51)
Chapter seven takes up the "eschatological nature" of the church (*eschatology* is the study of the "last things," the final destiny of human beings and of the whole world). It began as a chapter on the saints, inserted in the summer of 1964 at the request of Paul VI, who wanted to honor John XXIII's request that the Council say something about the saints. But when the chapter was debated at the third session, many bishops complained that it was too individualistic. And so it was revised to emphasize more clearly the eschatological nature of the church itself. We are not just a collection of individual pilgrims. We are a pilgrim people, still "on the way" to the reign of God. The recogni-

tion that the church "will receive its perfection only in the glory of heaven" (*LG,* 48) tempers the triumphalism of the past.

CHAPTER EIGHT: THE BLESSED VIRGIN MARY (*LG,* 52–69)

One of the closest votes of the entire Council was whether Mary should be treated in a document all her own or whether she should be treated within the document on the church. Behind this question were two differing, and deeply held, convictions about Mary. On the one hand were those adopting a more *Christ-centered* approach, which emphasized Mary's closeness to Christ and her powerful role in his work of salvation. They wanted a separate document for Mary. On the other hand were those with a more *church-centered* approach, which emphasized Mary's relationship to the community of believers and her role as first among the disciples. They wanted Mary to be included in the document on the church.

When the Council voted 1,114 to 1,074 to include Mary in the constitution on the church (October 29, 1963), the drafters were left with the challenge of balancing these two approaches. And the final chapter is marked by the tension of holding them together. For example, advocates of the Christ-centered approach lobbied that the title "mediatrix of all graces" be applied to Mary in the chapter. The other side resisted the title on scriptural grounds and for ecumenical reasons. So the decision was made to include it, but only as one among several other traditional titles used for Mary. And, immediately afterward, a clear statement was made that this takes nothing away from the unique role of Christ as the one mediator between God and humanity (*LG,* 62).

APPENDIX: THE PRELIMINARY NOTE OF EXPLANATION

LG ends with a long footnote *(nota praevia explicativa)* added to the text in the eleventh hour by the Theological Commission at the request of "higher authority" (presumably Pope Paul VI). It sought to clarify the meaning of collegiality, treated in chapter three, by stating that (1) the word "college" does not imply a group of equals in the legal sense,

(2) one enters this college *both* through episcopal ordination *and* hierarchical communion with the pope, (3) there is no such thing as the college of bishops without its head, the pope, and (4) the pope retains the right to exercise his power at any time. This note did not change the teaching spelled out in chapter three. But with it Paul VI clearly meant to satisfy the complaints of the small, but vocal minority of bishops who did not want to see papal primacy jeopardized. Many of the bishops were disappointed by this move. The fact that this note had been imposed on the text by the pope, without debate or a vote by all the bishops, seemed to contradict the spirit of the Council. Because of this move the third session ended on a gloomy note.

THE DOCUMENT TODAY
MODELS OF THE CHURCH
Shortly after the Council, the American Jesuit Avery Dulles wrote an influential book called *Models of the Church*. In it he argued that many of the disagreements people have about issues *in the church* can be traced back to their differing visions *of the church*. People who disagree often have different models of what the church is and ought to be. Dulles identified five models: institution, mystical communion, herald, sacrament and servant. (Dulles later added a sixth, community of disciples, as a kind of supermodel.)

The dominant model of the church from the Reformation to Vatican II was the model of the church as an *institution*. The church was envisioned primarily as a visible society, with emphasis on its hierarchical structures. *LG* knocked this institutional model of the church off its pedestal. Rather than offer a once-and-for-all definition of the church, *LG* described the church as a mystery. Instead of imposing one model, it suggested a variety of images for the church. No one image says everything there is to say about the church, but each image says something, each highlights some aspect of the mystery.

PEOPLE OF GOD AND THE CHURCH AS A COMMUNION
Not everyone was satisfied with *LG*'s juxtaposition of various images of the church. They sought in the council texts some unifying princi-

ple, some organizing idea behind the Council's many proposals. Commentators immediately afterward identified "people of God" as the main theme of Vatican II and the new paradigm for ecclesiology. This theme highlighted the dynamic, developmental sense of the church as a people on pilgrimage. It also affirmed the equality of everyone in the church—clergy and laity—over and against the hierarchical slant of the institutional model. But by the 1980s, many theologians and church leaders were emphasizing the theme of the church as a "communion." The 1985 extraordinary synod of bishops went so far as to say that "the ecclesiology of communion is the central and fundamental idea of the council's documents." The model of communion highlights the spiritual and relational aspects of the church. It links horizontal communion among believers to vertical communion with God. And it emphasizes the Eucharist as the place where this twofold communion is actualized.

COLLEGIALITY IN GENERAL

By declaring the doctrines of papal primacy and papal infallibility, the First Vatican Council (1869–1870) had so emphasized the role of the pope that all other bishops seemed superfluous. Vatican II sought to restore balance to the relationship between pope and bishops. And so it introduced the notion of collegiality, which, in a strict sense, refers to the sharing of authority among bishops and pope.

But "collegiality" can also be used in a more general sense, referring to the sharing of authority at all levels in the church. At the time of Vatican II, many welcomed the new emphasis on the role of the local bishop. But today some ask if there hasn't been too much emphasis on him. And there are voices calling for bishops to exercise their authority in more collegial ways—not by denying their divine mandate as shepherds of the flock, but by asking them to work more closely with the people they serve. Are there ways for bishops to share authority with the priests of the diocese? Are there ways for priests to share authority with the people of their parishes? Are there structures—such as diocesan or parish councils—that could be used more effectively to collaborate? Are there ways to ensure accountability from church leaders?

THE TEACHING OF THE CHURCH

Probably the most misunderstood teaching of the Catholic church is its teaching on papal infallibility. Ultimately, this doctrine is rooted in the ancient conviction that God would not let the church so veer off course that it would find itself in error on the basic truths necessary for salvation. Vatican II brought out more clearly how papal infallibility is meaningful only within the context of the infallibility that God gives to the whole church. Speaking of the supernatural "sense of the faith" by which believers intuitively know what is true, *LG* states: "The whole body of the faithful who have received an anointing which comes from the holy one (see 1 Jn 2:20 and 27) cannot be mistaken in belief" (*LG,* 12; see also *LG,* 35; *DV,* 8).

This recognition of the infallibility of the whole church does not deny the distinctive role of the pope and his brother bishops as the authoritative guardians of the faith. But it does challenge a simplistic understanding of the way in which the church teaches. Such an approach assumes a one-way street: The bishops teach something as true, and the laity accept and obey it. A more nuanced approach recognizes a circular, reciprocal relationship between bishops and the whole church: (1) a teaching or belief emerges first in the life of the community, among believers reflecting on their faith and expressing it in practices, worship and daily life; (2) bishops reflect on these practices and beliefs, assess them in light of the tradition and, if necessary, articulate teachings in an official way; (3) these official teachings are then received by the community, where they prompt further reflection and practice, and the cycle starts again.

THE HOLINESS OF THE CHURCH

Traditionally, the church has taught that, while its sons and daughters often sin, the church itself is sinless. (This is bound up in belief in the church's "indefectibility," its "inability to fail" in its mission.) The distinction is thus made between the holiness *of the church* and holiness *in the church*. And it explains *LG*'s claim that, while the church itself is "unfailingly holy," all of its members "are called to holiness" (*LG,* 39). Critics of this distinction charge that it frees the church's hierarchy from culpability and overlooks tragic examples of the church's failures (for example, the Crusades, the Inquisition, the sex-abuse scandal). Those who defend the distinction point out that church leaders—popes, bishops and priests—are also "sons" of the church. They sin too. The distinction is simply trying to affirm that the holiness of the church flows from Christ, who loved the church and left his Holy Spirit with it (*LG,* 39). And calling the church "unfailingly holy" does not prevent us from also recognizing that it will "receive its perfection only in the glory of heaven" (*LG,* 48).

FOR REFLECTION

• Read *LG,* 5–7: What images of the church resonate with you? Why? Think of one concrete, controversial issue in the church today. What does your position on this issue say about your vision of the church?

• Read *LG,* 1 and 9: Are you drawn more to the model of the church as people of God or church as communion? Are you drawn more to chapter one or chapter two of *LG?* Explain why and how you see them related.

• Read *LG,* 37: What are the areas of church life in your own parish or diocese that call for greater collaboration? What are the areas where you see successful collaboration taking place?

• Read *LG,* 12, 25 and 35: How do we know where the church is united in belief? What teachings do you see as essential to the faith? How does the reciprocal model described above function concretely? How should it function?

• Read *LG,* 39 and 48: Compare chapters five and seven of *LG.* How does *LG* handle the question of sin and the church? Do you find the distinction between the holiness *of the church* and holiness *in the church* helpful? Why or why not?

4

....

Pastoral Constitution on the Church in the Modern World
Gaudium et Spes

Together, the Dogmatic Constitution on the Church and the Pastoral Constitution on the Church in the Modern World (*GS*) stand as the two pillars of the Second Vatican Council. The Dogmatic Constitution treats the *nature* of the church in itself; the Pastoral Constitution treats its *mission* in the world.

A Plan for the Whole Council

GS began with a conversation between Pope John XXIII and Archbishop (soon to be Cardinal) Suenens of Belgium in March of 1962. While discussing the upcoming Council, Suenens complained about the number of drafts being prepared—over seventy different documents. How would the Council move through all this material? No one seemed to be thinking of the big picture. No one had a plan for how all of these topics would be organized, prioritized and actually debated by the assembly. He concluded, "It will be total chaos!" Reflecting on Suenens's observation, the pope asked him, "Would you like to make a plan?"

....

Pastoral Constitution on the Church in the Modern World
Preface
Introduction: The Condition of Humanity in the World Today
Part One: The Church and the Human Vocation
Chapter One: The Dignity of the Human Person
Chapter Two: The Human Community
Chapter Three: Humanity's Activity in the Universe
Chapter Four: Role of the Church in the Modern World
Part Two: Some More Urgent Problems
Chapter One: The Dignity of Marriage and the Family
Chapter Two: Proper Development of Culture
Chapter Three: Economic and Social Life
Chapter Four: The Political Community
Chapter Five: Fostering of Peace and Establishment of a Community of
  Nations
Conclusion: Role of Individual Christians and of Local Churches

....

Cardinal Suenens took up the pope's request immediately. He developed a two-part plan: The Council should consider both the church in its inner life *(ad intra)* and the church in its relationship to the outside world *(ad extra)*. Everything the Council said could then be arranged under these two categories. Suenens shared his proposal with Pope John and a small group of cardinals (including the future Pope Paul VI, Cardinal Montini) and waited for the right moment to make this plan public.

That moment came on December 4, 1962. Toward the end of the Council's first session—with frustration spreading because of the Council's slow pace and with Pope John's health in decline—Suenens rose to address the assembly. He urged his brother bishops not only to focus on the church in and of itself, but also to examine the church's relationship to the world at large. His remarks were followed by sustained applause from the assembly. The next day Cardinal Montini seconded Suenens's proposal. The seed of *GS* was planted.

A DOCUMENT WITHOUT A NAME

The Council did not follow through on all aspects of Suenens's master plan, but after his speech it was clear that a new document on the church in the modern world was necessary. In January of 1963 the Coordinating Commission (the central clearinghouse for work being done by the different conciliar commissions) added this item at the end of their seventeen-point agenda. And so the new document earned the nickname "Schema 17." ("Schema" was the generic term for a draft document.) A year and a half later the agenda was reordered, and the document took the "unlucky" working title "Schema 13."

To call the history of Schema 13 complicated is an understatement. No document of Vatican II changed so radically, so many times, as this one. The drafting commissions had no model for this kind of text. They were caught between trying to write something both doctrinal and pastoral, both biblical and philosophical, both general and particular, both traditional and contemporary. Dozens of drafts—with at least four complete rewrites—occupied consultations ranging across Europe and stretching almost three years.

A draft (written in large part by the moral theologian Bernard Häring) was eventually ready for debate at the Council's third session. The response was generally positive, although the discussion produced a long list of suggestions for revision. One of the chief difficulties was the twofold division of the document. The draft had evolved into a main text followed by a series of appendices on (1) the human person in society, (2) marriage and family, (3) culture, (4) economic and social life, and (5) the community of nations and peace. The relation of the main text to the appendices was unclear. Were the appendices part of the document or not? If not, what authority did they have? If so, why weren't they debated? Some felt that an ecumenical Council shouldn't treat issues that are too contemporary or constantly changing, while others argued that that was the whole point! Following the third session, this arrangement was scrapped and the appendices were incorporated as full chapters in "Part Two" of the main text.

"TOOTHING STONES"

Between the third and fourth sessions of the Council, Schema 13 underwent another complete rewrite. The revisions were done by a French sociologist and priest named Pierre Haubtmann. But the approach was really inspired by the French Dominican Marie-Dominique Chenu. For years Chenu had been calling the church to read the "signs of the times." The church must seek points of contact between Christianity and the modern world. He used the image of "toothing-stones" *(pierres d'attente)* that jut out from the end of a building or wall in anticipation of an addition. The church must find the "toothing-stones" in the world—areas of common concern where the church could "latch on" and begin to dialogue with contemporary people.

After further debate and final revisions during the fourth session of the Council, the Pastoral Constitution on the Church in the Modern World was approved and promulgated on December 7, 1965—one of the last (and by far the longest) documents of Vatican II.

NEW FISSURES

The debates on liturgy and revelation at the Council's first session revealed a split between a large number of bishops open to church reform and a small number opposed to it. Commentators quickly characterized this division as a battle between a progressive majority and a conservative minority. And, in many ways, this characterization was true. But what this way of framing the debate missed was the real diversity within each of these groups. As the Council moved on to debate other issues, the simple division into two camps didn't always work. For example, the "progressive" Suenens sounded like a conservative in his speech on Mary. The "conservative" Ottaviani sounded liberal in his condemnation of modern warfare.

The debate on Schema 13 is a case in point. The French text inspired by Chenu was severely criticized as overly optimistic by some of the German-speaking theologians at the Council (including a young Joseph Ratzinger, who would become Pope Benedict XVI). The search for toothing-stones, they claimed, overlooked the power of sin in the world. Besides, it obscured the distinctive nature of the Christian message. Instead of seeking out the lowest common denominator, the document should present the gospel in all its truth and beauty. Emphasis should not be on *dialoguing* with the world, but *proclaiming* Christ to it.

These were deep disagreements *within* the progressive majority. Both sides were in favor of church reform and renewal, but they had different ideas about how this should be accomplished. And these differences would have a profound impact on the way in which *GS* would be interpreted in the years after the Council.

READING GUIDE

GS begins not with the Bible or church doctrine. It begins with the world, with its joys and hopes *(Gaudium et Spes),* its grief and anguish. The document's two parts seek to respond to these lights and shadows, these questions and concerns, of the world in our time. Part One offers general principles for a Christian anthropology (a theological vision of the human person). Part Two takes up five urgent problems.

PREFACE AND INTRODUCTION (*GS*, 1–10)
The Human Person as the Key (*GS*, 1–3)

The Preface addresses *GS* to all people and expresses the church's desire to dialogue with the whole human family. Such a dialogue demands a common language, which is found by focusing on the human person. Here, *GS* finds a toothing-stone on which to build: The dignity of the human person is a point of contact between the concerns of the world and the concerns of the church.

The Signs of the Times (*GS*, 4–10)

The Introduction turns to read the "signs of the times," briefly describing some of the features of the modern world. The overriding characteristic of the world today, the bishops claimed, is the reality of change. This change has social, moral and religious dimensions. *GS* sees the world caught up in profound transformations, deep shifts that have created imbalances among people. In a world marked by ambiguity, people crave "a life that is full, autonomous, and worthy of their nature as human beings" (*GS*, 9). But they seek something more: ultimate meaning. *GS* confidently proclaims that Christ is the meaning of human life and the key to human history.

PART ONE: THE CHURCH AND THE HUMAN VOCATION

The guiding question of Part One is: What does it mean to be a human person today? And each chapter follows a similar method: The "signs of the times" are read, common values are sought, and Jesus Christ is proclaimed (*GS*, 11).

CHAPTER ONE: THE DIGNITY OF THE HUMAN PERSON (*GS*, 12–22)

Made in the Image of God (*GS*, 12–18)

The dignity of the human person flows out of God's act of creating men and women "in the image of God." This theme guided the development of *GS* very early on. The image and likeness of God is marred through sin, but redeemed by Christ. It grants a dignity to the person that can be recognized in human intellect, conscience and freedom. The article on sin comes early (*GS*, 13), but is placed within an overwhelmingly positive affirmation of human nature.

Atheism (*GS*, 19–21)

Atheism is then named as one of the chief threats to the dignity of the human person. These articles are some evidence of the Council's long and difficult debate on the issue of atheism and atheistic communism in particular. In the early 1960s this was not just a theological issue; it was a political issue as well. Some favored dialogue with atheists.

Others—particularly those who had suffered under communist regimes—demanded an explicit condemnation of Marxism by name. Still others, fearful of reprisals by communist states, cautioned moderation. In the end "systematic atheism" was separated out from atheism in general. And the text uses condemnatory language but avoids an explicit condemnation.

Christ the New Man (GS, 22)

Each chapter of Part One ends with a section on Christ as the culmination of the church's contribution to dialogue with the world. Faced with the question of the meaning of human existence, GS proclaims unambiguously: Christ reveals what it means to be human.

CHAPTER TWO: THE HUMAN COMMUNITY (GS, 23–32)

Chapter two turns from the *personal* dimension treated in chapter one to the *communal* dimension of human life. The chapter alternates between biblical principles (God creates people to be together; human community reflects trinitarian communion; we are called to be a neighbor to all and to love our enemies) and social principles (concern for the common good and the demands of justice). It makes explicit its reliance on the social encyclicals of John XXIII and Paul VI (GS, 23). Finally, the example of Christ's immersion in human society, his preaching and actions on behalf of others, is a call to us toward solidarity.

CHAPTER THREE: HUMAN ACTIVITY (GS, 33–39)

This chapter takes up the advancement of human technology and society and considers the role of human work in all of this. It affirms the value of human labor as a continuation of the work of the Creator (GS, 34), but stresses that human activity ought to be for the benefit of human beings: "People are of greater value for what they are than for what they have" (GS, 35). All activity is perfected through love, a love exemplified in the paschal mystery of Christ. And the world's activity reaches its culmination in the world to come (GS, 39).

Women at the Council

For all its progressive thrust, Vatican II had little to say about women. Only a dozen or so specific references to women can be found in the council texts. In fact, only a few women actually played an official role at the Council. Lay observers were invited to the Council's second session, but they were all men. It was not until Cardinal Suenens reminded the assembly of this oversight that it even became an issue. ("Unless I am mistaken," Suenens said, "women make up one half of the world's population.") He called for an increase in the number of lay observers and asked that women be included among them.

And so it was that Paul VI invited a select group of women to the third and fourth sessions of Vatican II. In all, twenty-three women served as official *auditrices* ("listeners"), including three Americans: Mary Luke Tobin, President of the Conference of Major Religious Superiors of Women; Catherine McCarthy, President of the National Council of Catholic Women; and Claudia Feddish, a member of the Ukrainian Byzantine Rite and Superior General of the Sisters of Saint Basil the Great. Paul VI called theirs a "symbolic presence" at the Council. But these women were not passive spectators. They submitted proposals, coordinated informal meetings, and took part in meetings of the commissions on the laity and on the church in the modern world. But despite intense lobbying, no woman was allowed to formally address the full assembly of bishops.

CHAPTER FOUR: ROLE OF THE CHURCH IN THE WORLD (*GS*, 40–45)
Chapter four draws on the first three chapters of *GS* to reflect explicitly on the mutual interaction of church and world. Drawing heavily on *LG,* it offers a concise ecclesiology that highlights the image of the church as a leaven in the world, "the soul of human society in its renewal by Christ and transformation into the family of God" (*GS,* 40), and as a

sacrament "of communion with God and of the unity of the entire human race" (*GS,* 42, see *LG* 1).

While the church exists *in* the world, the two enjoy a proper autonomy. The church is not a political party. Nor is it "committed to any one culture or to any political, economic or social system" (*GS,* 42). Instead, the church offers principles that it draws from revelation, which it believes can "help to make the human family and its history still more human" (*GS,* 40). In addition, the church recognizes all that it has received *from* the world, from the advancement of the sciences, human cultures and the insights of various peoples (*GS,* 44). The text calls on the laity not to shirk their responsibilities in the world, but rather to allow their Christian faith to permeate all they do. They should turn to the clergy for guidance and spiritual strength, but also "realize that their pastors will not always be so expert as to have a ready answer to every problem" (*GS,* 43).

Finally, the chapter recognizes the church's one purpose: "that the kingdom of God may come and the salvation of the human race may be accomplished" (*GS,* 45). Christ, the Word through whom all things are made, is also the goal of human history.

PART TWO: SOME URGENT PROBLEMS

A footnote attached to the Preface of *GS* points out that, although it consists of two parts, the Pastoral Constitution constitutes an organic unity. The more doctrinal (theoretical) Part One does not overlook pastoral (practical) implications. And the more pastoral Part Two does not overlook the doctrinal foundations.

CHAPTER ONE: MARRIAGE AND THE FAMILY (*GS*, 47–52)

This chapter was one of the most hotly debated of the entire document. It took up issues that had a new urgency in the early 1960s, as the traditional institution of marriage in the West faced what seemed to be an onslaught of change coming from all directions—politics, culture, science, even theology itself! Debate in the council hall revolved around two issues:

The Nature of Marriage (GS, 47–48)

Traditional Catholic teaching described marriage according to its purposes, or "ends." Marriage was for (1) the procreation of children and (2) the well-being and relationship of the spouses—*and in that order*. The former was called the "primary end" of marriage, the latter the "secondary end." When a conflict between these two arose, the relationship of the spouses had to yield to the primary purpose of marriage: procreation. But the Council deliberately refused to use this primary/secondary distinction, speaking instead of love and fruitfulness as the two ends of marriage, without subordinating one to the other. This was a genuine advance in church teaching, and it followed a more basic shift—evident in this chapter—from a legalistic view of marriage as a *contract* to a more personal, biblical view of marriage as a *covenant*.

Birth Control (GS, 49–51)

The invention of the birth control pill led many Catholics to wonder if the church's traditional prohibition of artificial contraception would change. In June of 1964 Pope Paul VI identified a special commission set up to advise him on this issue. He reserved any final decision on the matter to himself, thus taking birth control off the Council's agenda. Therefore, *GS* could only make general statements. It offered a balanced treatment that affirmed *both* the moral right of couples to decide on the number of children to have *and* the obligation to make such a decision in light of objective moral criteria. Four years later Paul VI issued the encyclical *Humanae Vitae* (July 29, 1968), which reaffirmed the church's ban on artificial contraception. (At the same time, it allowed for certain forms of "natural" birth regulation, which includes what is today called Natural Family Planning.)

Chapter Two: Development of Culture (GS, 53–62)

The second chapter lays out general principles to guide the church's relationship to culture (defined broadly as all that goes toward "the

What's in a Name?

Church documents are usually cited by the first words of the Latin text. Thus the Pastoral Constitution on the Church in the Modern World is often called *Gaudium et Spes* for its opening words, "The joys and hopes...". But the document could easily have been known as *Gaudium et luctus* ("Joys and sorrows"). An earlier version of the document began with this contrasting pair. But the words in the first sentence were rearranged. The reason? *Gaudium* was biblical, *luctus* was not. Yet even with the change, the tension between the positive and negative aspects of human existence was not lost. The opening line continues, "The joys and hopes, the grief and anguish of the people of our time...".

refining and developing of humanity's diverse mental and physical endowments"). It repeats the emphasis on change in the modern world—change marked by both greater cultural unification and greater recognition of diversity. The church is concerned for culture because it follows the example of Christ, who entered into human society. Church and culture are related, but each enjoys legitimate autonomy. In the end, culture must serve the human person (*GS,* 59). This challenges Christians to recognize every person's right to culture and its benefits (*GS,* 60). The chapter ends with a remarkable call for more theological formation for laity and a freedom of inquiry and expression marked by both "humility and courage" (*GS,* 62).

CHAPTER THREE: ECONOMIC AND SOCIAL LIFE (*GS,* 63–72)

This chapter repeats its dependence on the growing body of Catholic social teaching—seen especially in papal encyclicals since the nineteenth century. The first line summarizes the two fundamental principles of this teaching: (1) the dignity of the human person and (2) the welfare of society as a whole. All economic decisions must respect these two principles. Thus economic development is not to be aimed at an increase in profits or greater production, but its goal is to be at the service of humanity in its totality—economic decisions are to serve people, not the bottom line (*GS,* 64). *GS'*s affirmation of the right to private property is conditioned by the deeper claim that the world's goods belong to all (*GS,* 69, 71). The huge economic inequalities among people of the world are to be brought to an end (*GS,* 66), particularly in the case of land reform desperately needed in the developing world (*GS,* 71). Labor takes precedence over capital; workers have a right to unionize and the right to a wage that allows for a dignified livelihood (*GS,* 67, 68).

CHAPTER FOUR: THE POLITICAL COMMUNITY (*GS,* 73–76)

Again laying out broad principles to be applied in a particular area of concern, *GS* here states that the political community exists for the common good (*GS,* 74). All citizens ought to be empowered to participate in the political process (*GS,* 75). The church, for its part, is not identified with any political party or even any one political system (*GS,* 76). Rather the church serves as the sign and safeguard of the transcendence of the human person. The church is witness to a truth that can have political implications for its members.

CHAPTER FIVE: PEACE AND THE COMMUNITY OF NATIONS (*GS,* 77–90)

Peace (GS, 77–78)

Inspired by John XXIII's encyclical *Pacem in Terris* (Peace on Earth)—issued just before his death—the final version of this chapter begins by describing peace as something more than the absence of war. Rather, peace is "the effect of righteousness," a harmony built into human society by God, a gift that flows from the peace of Christ but also a task that requires constant effort (*GS,* 78).

Avoiding War (GS, 79–82)

The invention of the atomic bomb, the Soviet incursions into Eastern Europe and the arms race of the Cold War marked the immediate context for the Council's debates on modern warfare. Some bishops argued that modern war's potential for total devastation had made traditional Catholic discussions of "just war" irrelevant. They called for a

The Pope and the United Nations

The debate on Schema 13 at the fourth session of Vatican II was overshadowed by Pope Paul VI's address to the General Assembly of the United Nations, demonstrating his genuine commitment to world peace. On October 4, 1965, he delivered his powerful call: "Never again war!" It was a truly ground-breaking trip. The day he returned to Rome, the Council began debate on the chapter of Schema 13 dealing with peace and the community of nations.

condemnation of modern war in all circumstances—following the prophetic vision of Pope John's *Pacem in Terris*. Others, particularly bishops from the United States and Great Britain, sought to avoid such a blanket condemnation. (Cardinal Francis Spellman of New York complained of the draft's "pacifist tendencies.") In the end, *GS* called the indiscriminate destruction of whole cities or areas "a crime against God and humanity"—the strongest condemnation of the entire Council (*GS*, 80). And it described the arms race itself as "one of the greatest curses on the human race" (*GS*, 81). At the same time, it recognized the legitimate right of nations to their own self-defense (*GS*, 79).

The International Community (GS, 83–90)

The discussion of war concludes with *GS* endorsing the idea of a universally recognized international body with the necessary authority to serve the cause of peace. There is found a strong call for greater international cooperation in addressing the root causes of war, especially economic injustices. The chapter ends with the proposal to create an organization of the universal church dedicated to promoting the cause of social justice around the world. This proposal took concrete shape after the Council in the establishment of the Vatican Secretariat for Justice and Peace.

CONCLUSION (GS, 91–93)

GS ends the way it begins, with an appeal to the whole world. It invites dialogue, both within the church and beyond its boundaries, on the proposals it presents—proposals that *GS* admits are only a beginning.

THE DOCUMENT TODAY

DIALOGUE OR PROCLAMATION?

The first question *GS* raises for us is one of methodology. The debate between the French and German advisers who worked on *GS* basically boiled down to method: Should the church *dialogue* with the world or *proclaim* Christ to it?

❝ For the ties which unite the faithful together are stronger than those which separate them: let there be unity in what is necessary, freedom in what is doubtful, and charity in everything **❞** (GS, 92).

Clearly one can do both. The difference is one of emphasis. And this difference continues to shape Catholic theology today. Proponents of "correlational theology" emphasize the need to dialogue. They see theology as a mutually enlightening and mutually critical conversation between one's religious tradition and the contemporary situation. Proponents of "kerygmatic theology" (from the Greek *kerygma*, meaning "proclamation") seek instead to proclaim the faith in its totality and beauty. They are not as concerned with dialogue. Truth, they believe, speaks for itself. The first approach presumes a positive evaluation of the world, created good by a loving God; the second is more conscious of the corruption brought by sin. The first highlights the Incarnation, the second the cross. (Some have characterized this debate as a division between followers of Saint Thomas Aquinas—who held a positive view of grace working in the world—and followers of Saint Augustine—who had a much more negative view of sin's power.)

SIGNS OF THE TIMES

In its Introduction *GS* offers a brief description of the modern world. But the perspective is primarily European, male and shaped by the realities of the early 1960s. While the larger principles articulated in *GS* remain valid, the "signs of the times" have changed. Many of the specific issues that occupied Vatican II have been replaced by new concerns. We in the West today worry not so much about atheism as about religious fundamentalism. The Cold War has given way to a war on terror. The role of women has taken on increased importance.

Modern Issues, Modern Languages

GS was the only Council text composed entirely in a modern language, French. While it was translated into Latin for debate in the council hall, bishops were provided with versions of the text in the main European languages. This had not been done for any of the other documents.

Environmental concerns are raised more forcefully. And we have an even greater appreciation for the diversity of peoples, the downsides of technology and the negative implications of the free market.

Marriage and Society

GS marked a breakthrough for official Catholic teaching on sex and marriage. Its recovery of the biblical language of covenant and its emphasis on the inter-personal dimension of the spousal relationship blew fresh air into an approach to marriage that had become stiflingly legalistic. Following the council, many theologians embraced GS's positive vision. They spoke of love and of the goodness of sex in marriage. Pope John Paul II himself celebrated sexual intercourse as the culmination of the husband and wife's gift of themselves to one another.

In recent years a new generation of Catholic theologians has begun to ask: What does all of this mean for the larger society in which marriage finds itself? These theologians—many of whom are raising families themselves—fear a romanticization of married love that can turn the family in on itself, ignoring the rest of the world. And they are seeking ways to resist negative trends in family life: the isolation created by the suburban home, increased family fragmentation, divorce, social networks that keep us from meeting people who are different from us, the power of a consumerism that threatens to shape all aspects of family life. Their concern is not so much society's responsibility for the family, but the family's responsibility for society. Simply talking about the beauty of married love is not enough. What is needed is a realistic appreciation for the "work" that marriage requires, as well as concrete practices that help foster among children and parents a concern for justice and the common good.

CHURCH AND STATE

GS states that Christ did not give the church a political mission. The purpose he gave it was religious. But, the document continues, this religious mission can be the source of commitment and direction in the effort to build a better world (*GS*, 42).

> **❝** To follow Christ the perfect human is to become more human oneself **❞** (*GS*, 41).

In the United States we are used to framing this discussion within the context of the establishment clause of the First Amendment, which we often reduce to the "separation of church and state." But separation does not imply that there is no interaction. Catholic citizens are involved in all levels of government. And the church's leaders—primarily through the statements and activities of the U.S. bishops' conference—have developed what could be called a political agenda, whose priorities include a range of issues: abortion, agricultural policies, capital punishment, education, foreign aid, health care, human rights, immigration reform, military spending, urban poverty and values in the media, among others. In addressing individual Catholics, the bishops' conference does not tell people how to vote; the bishops recognize that their role is not to endorse or oppose candidates. Instead, they call all Catholics to examine candidates on the full range of issues and to base their decisions on faith and moral convictions. In addressing the larger society, the bishops recognize that they cannot impose their beliefs on non-Catholics. But they claim that they—indeed all Catholics—have a responsibility to make their case in the public sphere by appealing to arguments based on the fundamental dignity of the human person, the importance of the common good and society's responsibility for the poor.

GLOBALIZATION

GS includes a few paragraphs on the reality of *change:* the modern world is marked by rapid and widespread change in almost every area of human life. This change, *GS* points out, has led to increasing inter-connectedness among people. At the same time, it has fed a growing imbalance between the rich and the poor.

The changes briefly described in *GS*—along with their positive and negative implications—have expanded at a rate and to an extent hard to imagine in 1965. "Globalization" has become *the* distinguishing feature of our time. What globalization means is often debated. Some champion it as the magic bullet that will end war, famine and ignorance across the globe. Others point out that the gap between rich and poor has only increased as a result of globalization. They see wealth and power held tightly by just a few nations and international corporations, and they call attention to the destruction of traditional customs and ways of life, not to mention the ecological devastation occurring all around the world. Most of the people who benefit from globalization, however, are largely unaware of or indifferent to these implications. Those who do care are often overwhelmed by the sheer complexity and size of the issues involved. They are paralyzed in any attempt to respond.

FOR REFLECTION

• Read *GS,* 2–3: How do dialogue and proclamation relate? Think in terms of catechesis: Should we emphasize the student's personal experience or focus on the content of the faith? Think in terms of the parish: Should the parish be a "public church," an active participant in the wider society? Or should it be a prophetic community set apart from contemporary culture, offering an alternative vision and a distinctive way of life?

• Read *GS,* 4–10: What do you see as the most important "signs of the times" today? What issues in the world demand our attention? What ways do the larger principles laid out in *GS* help in responding to these issues?

- Read *GS,* 47–52: What are the challenges facing spouses and families today? What specific actions can you take within your own family to meet these challenges?
- Read *GS,* 42, 73–76: What is the proper role of the church in politics? What role is played by different members of the church (laity and clergy)? When does the church go too far? When does it not go far enough?
- Read *GS,* 63–66, 83–90: How do you see globalization portrayed in the media? What is your own assessment? Evaluate the norms listed in *GS,* 86 and apply them to a concrete example of globalization.

PART TWO

....

THE CHURCH AS THE PEOPLE OF GOD

5

....

DECREE ON THE PASTORAL OFFICE OF BISHOPS IN THE CHURCH
Christus Dominus

The First Vatican Council (1869–1870) focused on the bishop of Rome, the pope, but it never got around to saying anything about the other bishops. Thus, when John XXIII called for a Second Vatican Council, everyone expected it to take up this unfinished business.

FOCUS ON PRACTICAL QUESTIONS

The work of drafting a document on bishops was hampered by a decision early on to separate doctrinal and disciplinary questions. One preparatory commission took up theory; another took up practice.

The Decree on the Pastoral Office of Bishops in the Church *(CD)* can be traced back to the preparatory commission on bishops—which was responsible for the *practical* issues. In the months leading up to Vatican II, this commission debated everything from reforming the Vatican bureaucracy (the curia) to mandating a retirement age for bishops. The commission produced seven different documents that were then reduced to two: "Bishops and the Government of Dioceses" and "The Care of Souls." Eventually, these were combined into a single document.

Decree on the Pastoral Office of Bishops in the Church

Introduction

Chapter One: The Bishops in Relation to the Universal Church

Chapter Two: Bishops in Relation to Their Own Churches or Dioceses

Chapter Three: Concerning the Cooperation of Bishops for the Common Good of a Number of Churches

How to Be Collegial

In early November 1963, debate on "Bishops and the Government of Dioceses" began. But the heavy lifting had already been done. Just a few days earlier (October 30), a straw vote had revealed strong support for the principle of collegiality (the idea that the pope shares authority with his brother bishops). And so, many speakers demanded that the draft on bishops better reflect this principle. This was part of a larger call for decentralization in the church. Many wanted the rights of local bishops emphasized. Other wanted to see regional bishops' conferences affirmed. Still others called for a permanent senate of bishops, a representative group elected by bishops from around the world, who would assist the pope in governing the universal church. All of these were attempts to escape the monarchical view of the church that had taken hold since Vatican I.

Some of the more pointed critiques were directed at the Vatican curia, which had become a symbol of all the problems with centralization —for here a few well-placed officials exercised enormous and often unchecked power. Cardinal Josef Frings of Cologne aimed his attack at the Holy Office (the curia office responsible for questions of doctrine, now called the Congregation for the Doctrine of the Faith). He called the procedures of the Holy Office—its arbitrary decisions, its condemnations without hearings, its judgments without appeal—a scandal to the world. This prompted a passionate defense by Cardinal Ottaviani, the head of the Holy Office. He said that to attack the Holy Office was to attack the pope himself. He doubted the legitimacy of the October 30 vote, and even questioned the principle of collegiality itself. But his desperate appeal only revealed how much the tide was turning.

After the second session, the document was completely recast. The new text adopted the principle of collegiality as its guiding theme. After further revisions, *CD* was formally approved at the Council's fourth session (October 28, 1965).

> **"** Bishops, in the exercise of their teaching office, are to proclaim to humanity the gospel of Christ. This is one of their principal duties **"** (*CD*, 12).

READING GUIDE

CD depends on the theology of the episcopate developed in chapter three of the Constitution on the Church (*LG*) and cannot be understood apart from it. The Introduction of *CD* follows *LG*'s traditional view of apostolic succession: The pope and the other bishops take the place of the apostles, who were sent out by Christ the Lord *(Christus dominus)*. But *CD*'s Introduction also notes the two "new" teachings of *LG*: the collegiality of bishops and the sacramentality of episcopal consecration.

CD describes how bishops exercise their office at three levels: in the universal church (chapter one), in their own "particular church" or diocese (chapter two), and at the regional or national level (chapter three).

CHAPTER ONE: BISHOPS IN THE UNIVERSAL CHURCH (*CD*, 4–10)

It is significant that *CD* treats the universal and missionary responsibilities of the bishop before it treats his leadership role in the diocese. Chapter one suggests a synod of bishops, selected from around the world, as one concrete way in which bishops could act together in caring for the universal church (*CD*, 5). The Roman Curia ought to be reorganized so that it can better accomplish its true purpose: serving the bishops. Its membership should represent the worldwide church, and laypeople should be consulted (*CD*, 9–10).

....

The Synod of Bishops

In his speech opening the Council's fourth session, Pope Paul VI announced his intention to create a worldwide synod of bishops. The next day (September 15, 1965), the council secretary read the pope's letter *Apostolica Sollicitudo,* which gave the synod its legal form. This surprise gesture cheered many at the Council who were still disillusioned by the third session's gloomy end. But the enthusiasm was short-lived.

In previous debates several speakers had proposed a synod of bishops as one way to enact the Council's teaching on collegiality. They envisioned the synod as a permanent deliberative body that would share in the pope's governing of the church. But *Apostolica Sollicitudo* offered a more modest vision. It introduced the synod not as a "bottom-up" organ of the world's bishops but as a "top-down" instrument of the pope. Since Vatican II, synods have played only a consultative role. The timing, agenda and final document are decided by the pope and the Vatican curia. Many bishop participants have complained that the process obstructs the purpose: They feel they have little voice in an institution intended to give them one.

....

CHAPTER TWO: BISHOPS IN THEIR OWN DIOCESES (*CD,* 11–35)

In the diocese, or "particular church," the "one, holy, catholic and apostolic church of Christ is truly present and active" (*CD,* 11). At work here is a model of church drawn from early Christianity. In early Christianity the focus of attention was not on the universal church led by the pope (an emphasis of the Middle Ages), nor the parish led by the priest (a post-Reformation emphasis), but the diocese led by the bishop. Thus, *CD*'s chapter two is held in tension with the more universal vision of chapter one.

A veritable "job description" of the bishop follows, built around the threefold work of Christ as prophet, priest and king: The bishop proclaims the Word, sanctifies the people and shepherds his flock (*CD,*

12–16). Chapter two gives guidelines for redrawing diocesan boundaries, a concern at the time due to population shifts (*CD, 22–24*). A list of the bishop's collaborators includes: auxiliary (assistant) bishops, coadjutor bishops (auxiliaries who will succeed the current bishop), the diocesan curia and councils, clergy and religious (*CD, 25–35*). The lay apostolate is treated earlier (*CD, 17*). The need for dialogue, integration and a spirit of collaboration is underscored.

CHAPTER THREE: BISHOPS AND THE COMMON GOOD OF MANY CHURCHES (*CD, 36–44*)
Chapter three considers an intermediate level between the local diocese and the universal church. It briefly mentions regional synods and councils (*CD, 36*). It then proposes episcopal conferences as a promising way for bishops of a nation or region to collaborate. Episcopal conferences first emerged in the nineteenth century, and Vatican II affirmed their value. *CD* offers general guidelines for their establishment (*CD, 37–38*).

THE DOCUMENT TODAY
BISHOPS CONFERENCES
Since Vatican II national conferences of bishops have become an important way for bishops to exercise their teaching ministry. In the 1980s, the U.S. National Conference of Catholic Bishops (now the USCCB) issued successful documents on peace and on the economy. These involved a wide consultative process and were well-received both within and outside of the church. Since then, Rome has placed limits on the authority of bishops' conferences. A 1998 letter of Pope John Paul II stated that conferences can issue binding doctrinal statements only if a document is (1) approved unanimously by the bishops of the conference or (2) approved by a two-thirds majority and subsequently approved by Rome.

Some argue that strong episcopal conferences are necessary to tackle problems that individual bishops do not have the resources to handle. Others fear in these conferences a kind of nationalism or a bureaucratization of the bishops' role. Committees and consensus, they claim, undercut the prophetic edge of the gospel.

ELECTING BISHOPS

In the aftermath of recent scandals, many Catholics have begun to demand greater accountability from their bishops. Some even suggest that local clergy and laypeople should play a role in selecting their bishop. This call for democratic process has been dismissed by some as a modern innovation. But the truth is that the pope's practice of personally appointing bishops is a relatively recent development (a development that came largely in response to the encroachment of secular authorities into church affairs). For much of the church's history, local churches—especially local clergy—played a much greater role in choosing their bishop. Pope Leo the Great (c. 440–461) famously wrote of bishops: "He who is to preside over all must be elected by all."

FOR REFLECTION

• Read *CD*, 37–38: What do you see as the advantages and disadvantages of national bishops' conferences?

• Read *CD*, 20: Describe the potential dangers of electing bishops. How would you design a process of local involvement or selection that would avoid these dangers?

6

....

DECREE ON THE MINISTRY AND LIFE OF PRIESTS
Presbyterorum Ordinis
Preparations for Vatican II all but overlooked the role of priests in the church. Bishops and laity received all the attention. Priests got lost in the middle. But over the course of the Council, many of the participants called for greater attention to this important ministry. And the result was the Decree on the Ministry and Life of Priests *(PO)*.

A PASTORAL VISION
A document "On Clerics" was prepared in advance of the Council, but it only dealt with minor points of canon law. And it presupposed the cultic model of priesthood that had dominated Catholic thought for centuries. This cultic model saw the priest as a sacred figure, a mediator between God and humanity. His whole identity revolved around offering the sacrifice of the Mass on behalf of the people. Thus the priest was "set apart" from others—called to a special and more perfect state of holiness.

The bishops at the Council demanded that the text give more attention to the broader pastoral ministry of the priest. The Eucharist is an important element of the priest's ministry—but so too is preaching, so too is his leadership within the community. Subsequent drafts were recast with this in mind. The document also moved away from an individualistic focus on the priest's spiritual life. The final text gives more attention to the various relationships that shape the priest's ministry.

WE NEED TO SAY SOMETHING

In early 1964 the drafting and redrafting of this document was interrupted by instructions from the Coordinating Commission to cut it down to a few summary points. This was part of a larger plan that involved drastically reducing several documents in order to bring the Council to a quick conclusion. Therefore, what the bishops received at the third session was the mere skeleton of a document. And they didn't like it. There was a growing fear among many bishops that their priests would feel neglected if the Council did not say something substantive and encouraging to them. And so the draft was roundly criticized as being too short to do justice to the subject matter—the skeleton needed to be fleshed out.

Since several other shortened documents hung in the balance, this debate was watched with great interest. When the assembly voted to reject the text and send it back to committee, any hope of ending Vatican II that fall disappeared. Many of the other short documents were similarly rejected. A fourth session of the Council was planned.

BUT NO DEBATE ON CELIBACY

At the fourth session, a greatly expanded and much-improved document on priests was presented to the assembly. A few days before debate began, Archbishop Felici read a letter from Pope Paul VI that effectively took the issue of priestly celibacy off the table. The pope said the time was not ripe to discuss ordaining married men. This announcement disappointed many of the bishops—particularly those from Latin America—who had hoped that the Council would reconsider the issue in light of current pastoral needs. But the pope's decision did keep a potentially divisive issue from stalling progress on the document. The revised draft was approved a few days later. After minor revisions, *PO* was formally promulgated on December 7, 1965.

> **❝** Through the ministry of priests, the spiritual sacrifice of the faithful is completed in union with the sacrifice of Christ the only mediator **❞** (*PO, 2*).

READING GUIDE

The Introduction to *PO* notes that the Second Vatican Council treats the order of priests *(presbyterorum ordinis)* in several other places. Therefore, we benefit by reading this document along with the documents on liturgy, bishops, priestly training and, especially, the church (*LG, 28*).

PO's three chapters place the life of the priest (chapter three) in the context of the priest's ministry (chapter two), and the priest's ministry in the context of the mission of the whole church (chapter one).

CHAPTER ONE: THE PRIESTHOOD IN THE CHURCH'S MISSION (*PO, 2–3*)

The first chapter repeats a traditional cultic model of priesthood. It cites the Council of Trent (1545–1563) when it says that priests receive a "sacred power" for "offering sacrifice and forgiving sins" (*PO, 2*). But this cultic view is transformed in a new context. After all, chapter one treats the mission of the *whole* church. And the ordained priesthood is described only after the priesthood of all the faithful. In fact, the very goal and meaning of the ordained priesthood is precisely to help the priestly people of God exercise their priesthood—which consists in life lived as a spiritual sacrifice to God. Priests act in the person of Christ the Head, but all members of Christ's body share in the church's mission.

The chapter goes on to say that, although, in a certain sense, the priest is set apart, he is also thoroughly immersed in the people of God.

....

How to End a Council?

Vatican II began with no clear exit strategy. No one knew how long it would last. This was a concern to Paul VI, who was elected pope after the Council's first session. The new pope turned to Cardinal Julius Döpfner of Munich for help. Döpfner had already shown a keen eye for the internal workings of the Council. The pope asked him to develop a practical plan to bring Vatican II to a speedy and satisfactory conclusion.

Döpfner presented his plan after the close of the second session. Following the lead of Paul VI, his goal was to end Vatican II with a third session. To accomplish this, Döpfner called for a number of procedural changes to speed up the Council's work. He suggested reducing the minor documents on the agenda to a series of short propositions. The idea was that the bishops could then quickly vote on these propositions without lengthy debate. Thus the documents on religious life, eastern churches, missions, seminaries, Catholic education and the clergy were each drastically cut down to a few bullet points.

But at the third session, the "Döpfner Plan" fell apart. The bishops demanded time for debate. The shortened documents were judged inadequate. And the number of topics was still too large to treat in a few weeks. Even Döpfner himself doubted that the Council could complete all its work at the third session. Eventually, all of the short texts were fleshed out again and the Council met for a fourth and final session in 1965.

....

CHAPTER TWO: THE MINISTRY OF PRIESTS (*PO*, 4–11)

Priestly Functions (*PO*, 4–6)

Following the threefold work of Christ as prophet, priest and king, chapter two describes the priest's ministry of word, worship and leadership. Preaching is the first task of priests. This preaching finds its source and summit in the Eucharist. And, as a pastor, the priest is called to care for a variety of groups in his community, especially the poor and weak.

Relationships With Others (PO, 7–9)

PO abandons an individualistic conception of the priest. Instead, the priest is envisioned within a web of relationships that constitute the church.

Priests share with bishops the same priesthood and ministry of Christ. The text speaks of the need for collaboration, dialogue and mutual concern between priests and their bishops. They are to be "brothers and friends." But theologically, bishops enjoy the "fullness of the sacrament of order" (*PO,* 7). Prior to the Council, the bishop was defined in relation to the priest (the bishop was a priest with jurisdiction over a diocese). After the Council, the priest is defined in relation to the bishop.

The priest shares with other priests—particularly the priests of his diocese—a common cause (*PO,* 8). They should help one another and find ways to gather together regularly. Among laypeople the priest is a brother among brothers and sisters (*PO,* 9). The priest is a teacher, but he is a disciple first. And this he shares with all of the faithful. The priest must listen to the laity, foster their gifts, and entrust to them roles in service of the church.

A final section (*PO,* 10–11) emphasizes the universal mission of the priestly ministry and calls on all to promote vocations to the priesthood.

CHAPTER THREE: THE LIFE OF PRIESTS (*PO,* 12–21)

Called to Holiness (PO, 12–17)

Baptism calls everyone in the church to holiness. Priests are especially bound to this call, and their particular way of moving toward holiness lies precisely in the exercise of their ministry. Chapter three makes this point by adopting the priest's threefold ministry of word, worship and leadership (*PO,* 13) as the framework for describing his spiritual life. Running throughout is an emphasis on Christ as the model of holiness.

PO applies the evangelical counsels of obedience, chastity and poverty (*PO,* 15–17) to the particular circumstances of the priest. (The text clearly has all priests in mind, and not just those who belong to religious orders who formally profess these vows.) Since Pope Paul VI took priestly celibacy off the table, *PO* reiterates the traditional teaching. Celibacy is not demanded by the very nature of the priesthood (evidenced by the Eastern Catholic churches that allow for married priests). But the Council "approves and confirms this legislation" for the Roman Church (*PO,* 16).

To Help the Priest (*PO,* 18–22)

The main help for priests in living holy lives is their work of ministry. In addition, *PO* recommends several spiritual practices: reading Scripture, celebrating Eucharist, penance, visits to the Blessed Sacrament, retreats, spiritual direction and personal prayer (*PO,* 18). Ongoing education is stressed (*PO,* 19). And the document calls for just remuneration and adequate systems of social security for priests (*PO,* 20–21).

A final exhortation to priests concludes the document (*PO,* 22).

THE DOCUMENT TODAY

AN IDENTITY CRISIS

Despite all its problems, one thing could be said of the preconciliar cultic model of ministry: It was clear what it meant to be a priest. A priest was a man set apart for the things of God. He was elevated above the community and charged with the awesome task of offering the eucharistic sacrifice. But Vatican II pushed this model off its pedestal. And in its place came a variety of models emphasizing pastoral care. The priest was no longer a sacral figure, but a "servant leader."

Naturally, such a radical shift contributed to an identity crisis in the priesthood. In recent years, a new generation of priests has tried to counter this crisis by recovering aspects of the cultic model. These younger clergy members underscore the distinctiveness of the priest—enthusiastically embracing celibacy, doctrinal orthodoxy and traditional priestly garb. This movement has fostered enthusiasm and some limited success in attracting others to the priesthood. But studies show new problems as well. The young priests often clash with older priests who were formed in the servant-leader model. Also, lay ministers and other active parishioners experience these new priests as less open to collaboration.

> **"** Priests owe it to everybody to share with them the truth of the Gospel in which they rejoice in the Lord **"** (PO, 4).

FEWER AND FEWER PRIESTS

Sociological studies show that the number of active priests in the United States is declining at an alarming rate. Each year, American seminaries are producing only 35 to 45 percent of the priests needed to keep the priesthood at a constant size. On top of this, the American Catholic population continues to grow at a steady pace. Every indication suggests these trends will continue.

CELIBATE MEN

Two issues have generated significant debate since the Council: the requirement of celibacy for priests and the exclusion of women from ordained ministry.

Since the Council, the Vatican has repeatedly declared its support for mandatory celibacy. Nevertheless, there are some married priests in the Catholic church. Many belong to Eastern Catholic churches in union with Rome that allow for this practice. And exemptions have been made for a small number of married clergy who entered the Roman Catholic church after being ordained in the Episcopal church.

A 1976 Vatican document reaffirmed the church's traditional prohibition against the ordination of women to the priesthood. Pope John Paul II subsequently stated that this teaching must be "definitely held" by the faithful. Some theologians have suggested that this prohibition does not necessarily apply to deacons. They point to evidence of women deacons in the early church and suggest that ordaining women deacons today would allow for women to participate in the church's ordained ministry.

....

Priest or Presbyter?

The document on priests went through several titles:

"On Clerics" *(De Clericis)*

"On Priests" *(De Sacerdotibus)*

"On the Life and Ministry of Priests" *(De Vita et Ministerio Sacerdotali)*

"On the Ministry and Life of Presbyters" *(De Presbyterorum Ministerio et Vita)*

Each title change reflects a change in content. With the final title change we see two things. First, by reversing the order and treating the *ministry* of the priest before his *spiritual life*, the document implies that priestly spirituality must flow from the priest's service to the people of God. Second, by changing the more cultic term *sacerdotali* to the more pastoral term *presbyterorum*, the document moves away from a view of ministry exclusively focused on ritual to a view that includes a wide array of ministerial activities. (English translates both these words as "priests," and so we often miss this nuance. But the Latin *sacerdos* refers to a "cultic priest," someone who offers a sacrifice. The word *presbyteros* refers to an "elder," a leader in the community.)

....

FOR REFLECTION

• Read *PO,* 2–3: Reflect on the positives and negatives of a strong sense of the distinctiveness of priests.

• Read *PO,* 11: Why do so few young men enter seminary today? How do you see these trends impacting your own experience of church? What should be done about it? Is there any silver lining behind these statistics?

• Read *PO,* 16: How do you understand the arguments put forward for mandatory celibacy and for an all-male priesthood? How would you evaluate these arguments in light of the teachings of the Second Vatican Council?

....

DECREE ON THE TRAINING OF PRIESTS

Optatam Totius

The Decree on the Formation of Priests *(OT)* began as a sixty-page draft that called for the promotion of vocations and the reorganization of seminaries. By the time the bishops debated the document at the Council's third session, it had been trimmed to four pages. At least in this case, the old adage was true: "less is more."

The few critical voices raised in that debate came from those with the most to lose. The new text encouraged the decentralization of seminary education. No longer was universal uniformity the ideal. Bishops and bishops' conferences should set up their own programs of priestly formation. This didn't sit well with members of the Vatican's Congregation for Seminaries and Universities—who until then had called all the shots. Other suggestions in the text (for example, greater attention to practical ministerial preparation, openness to alternative theological approaches, efforts to avoid isolating seminarians from the world) pushed seminary education in new directions. This was resisted by a few, but embraced by many. The document was overwhelmingly approved at the third session. And, after a modest enlargement, the Decree on the Training of Priests was formally promulgated at the Council's fourth session (October 28, 1965).

Decree on the Training of Priests

1. Program of Priestly Formation in Different Countries
2. More Active Encouragement of Priestly Vocations
3. Major Seminaries
4. Greater Attention to Spiritual Training
5. The Revision of Ecclesiastical Studies
6. Strictly Pastoral Training
7. Ongoing Formation

READING GUIDE

The longed-for *(optatam)* renewal of the whole *(totius)* church depends, in large part, on priests. *OT* sets out general guidelines for reforming priestly training in order to achieve this goal of renewal. While addressing all priests, its focus is on diocesan clergy— revealing the persistent slant of the Council itself toward parish- and diocesan-based ministry (as distinct from the types of ministry historically provided by various religious orders, such as missionary activity, itinerant preaching, retreats and so on).

GENERAL PRINCIPLES AND LOCAL ADAPTATION (*OT*, 1–7)

The first section is the most important of the decree. Instead of the monolithic model of seminary education then in existence, *OT* encourages local episcopal conferences to develop their own programs of priestly formation attentive to the needs of their own churches (*OT*, 1).

OT then underscores the need to promote vocations to the priesthood (*OT*, 2). This is a duty of the whole community, from families to formal programs. Major seminaries (graduate-level education) play the primary role in preparing those men called to the priesthood (*OT*, 4–7).

HOLISTIC EDUCATION (*OT*, 8–21)

In addition to encouraging local adaptation, the second great contribution of *OT* is its holistic approach to seminary education. The document lays out three areas that need to be integrated in the formation of priests: the spiritual, intellectual and pastoral. *OT*'s vision of spiritual formation is thoroughly Christ-centered. It is sensitive to the psychological factors at play in the development of a healthy minister. In terms of intellectual formation, the document calls for a revision of seminary curricula. The goal is to better integrate philosophy and theology (*OT,* 14–15), to ensure a comprehensive engagement with the church's tradition (*OT,* 16), and to take advantage of new teaching methods (*OT,* 17). Notable is *OT*'s emphasis on the study of Scripture and its attention to other Christian communities and religions. While pastoral formation ought to permeate the whole formation process, special courses and programs should prepare future priests for the concrete exercise of their ministry (*OT,* 19–21). Practical field experience is encouraged.

❝ The entire training program is to be so organized that, with its atmosphere of piety, recollection and mutual support, it becomes a kind of initiation to the students' future lives as priests **❞** (*OT,* 11).

The document ends with a section encouraging the ongoing formation of priests (*OT,* 22) and a brief conclusion.

THE DOCUMENT TODAY

LAYPEOPLE IN SEMINARIES

After Vatican II, seminarians and other lay students began to mix in the classroom. On the one hand, Catholic colleges and universities launched degree programs in theology for laypeople. Some of these schools partnered with Catholic seminaries and Protestant divinity schools—exposing seminarians at these schools to a diverse student body. On the other hand, freestanding seminaries developed their own programs in lay ministry. At first, a few laymen and laywomen sat in classrooms full of men preparing for the priesthood. Now, the lay ministry students far outnumber the seminarians. These dynamics have challenged the very mission of the seminary as an institution. But at their best, these integrated programs instill a sense of collaboration and mutual understanding, preparing priests and lay ministers who can work together.

HEALTHY MINISTERS

The recent sexual abuse scandal drew new attention to the way in which seminaries screen candidates for the priesthood. Today seminarians go through an extensive process of personal, psychological and professional evaluation.

FOR REFLECTION

• Read *OT,* 8–21: Reflect on the ways in which you have been challenged to grow spiritually, intellectually and ministerially by people who are different than you.

• Read *OT,* 6, 11: What, in your opinion, are the characteristics of a healthy minister?

....

DECREE ON THE UP-TO-DATE RENEWAL OF RELIGIOUS LIFE
Perfectae Caritatis

Religious life is a vocation that involves communal living and the public profession of the vows of poverty, chastity and obedience. An early draft document on this topic was titled "On the States of Acquiring Perfection." The title hints at a static and legalistic treatment of religious life. Over the course of the Council, a more dynamic and spiritual vision of renewal emerged. This vision took shape in a new document with a new name: "The Decree on the Up-to-Date Renewal of Religious Life" *(PC)*.

SEEDS ARE PLANTED

The call for the renewal of religious life did not originate at Vatican II. Throughout the 1950s, Pope Pius XII had encouraged the adaptation of religious congregations to better meet the needs of the day. Conferences were held. Documents were issued. But even before this, the religious themselves were planting seeds. Already in the 1940s, women's communities were encouraging professional education for their sisters and nuns. This prepared a generation of women religious to respond to the Council's challenge with their own blend of careful reflection and unbridled enthusiasm—sparking a transformation of religious life on a scale that Pius XII, and even the Council itself, never imagined.

Decree on the Up-to-Date Renewal of Religious Life

This document is not divided into chapters, but comprises twenty-five articles.

RECOGNITION AND RETHINKING

The document on religious was debated at the Council's third session (November 10–12, 1964), at which several critiques were raised. Cardinal Döpfner of Munich argued that religious life needed to be radically rethought in light of the modern world. He accused the draft of missing this basic point. Instead of engaging the world, it simply repeated pious old phrases. Cardinal Suenens focused on women religious. He claimed that for too long the hierarchy had treated sisters and nuns like children. It was time to treat them like adults.

Voices of support for the draft were also raised, as were a variety of other issues. No consensus emerged, and the vote on the text was mixed. The document was basically approved. But there were so many amendments—over fourteen thousand—that the document had to be almost completely rewritten. A revised document that attempted to balance these many concerns was approved and promulgated at the Council's fourth session on October 28, 1965.

READING GUIDE

Jesus Christ provides the example of that perfect love *(perfectae caritatis),* which those in religious life seek through the evangelical counsels of chastity, poverty and obedience. The first line of *PC* reminds us that the Constitution on the Church offers the necessary foundation for this decree. (See *LG,* 6. Religious are also treated in *CD,* 33–35 and *AG,* 27, 32–33, 40.)

PRINCIPLES OF RENEWAL *(PC,* 1–6)

The renewal of religious life in the church is to be guided by two complementary movements: (1) a return to the sources of the Christian life, and in particular, the founding vision of each religious order, and (2) an adaptation to the changing conditions of our time *(PC,* 2). Thus religious communities since the Council have sought to recover their deepest traditions, to listen again to the original inspiration of their founding father or mother, and to allow that vision to guide them more explicitly. This "radical" move of returning to their roots has empowered these communities to find ways to be more relevant, to direct their energies toward the concrete needs of today.

> **"** Since the ultimate norm of the religious life is the following of Christ as it is put before us in the Gospel, this must be taken by all institutes as the supreme rule **"** (*PC*, 2).

Running through these opening paragraphs is a Christ-centered vision. Religious life is directed entirely toward following Christ, and the gospel is named as the supreme rule of every religious institute (*PC*, 2). The special divine call of religious is rooted in baptism (*PC*, 5), fed by love and nurtured through prayer (*PC*, 6).

TYPES OF RELIGIOUS LIFE (*PC*, 7–11)

A religious institute (also called a religious order or religious congregation) is a group of individuals who live together as brothers or sisters and who publicly profess the vows of chastity, poverty and obedience. While history has produced thousands of different kinds of religious institutes, they all share these two features: common life and vows. These groups are the focus of *PC*—although the document also includes "societies of common life" (which have a common life, but no vows) and "secular institutes" (which have vows, but no common life) (*PC*, 1).

Articles 7 through 11 treat several kinds of communities that have been important in the life of the church: institutes entirely devoted to contemplation (*PC*, 7), institutes dedicated to apostolic work (*PC*, 8), monasteries (*PC*, 9), groups of lay religious (*PC*, 10) and secular institutes (*PC*, 11). There is some overlap among these, but each type seemed worthy of affirmation by the council participants.

....

Up-to-Date Renewal

The official title of this decree (Decretum de Accommodata Renovatione Vitae Religiosae) has been variously translated as "On the Appropriate Renewal of Religious Life," "On the Sensitive Renewal," "The Adaptation and Renewal," and simply "Renewal." Behind these various attempts at translation is an effort to capture a twofold movement: a return to the sources and original inspiration of a religious order (renovatione) and an adaptation to contemporary needs (accommodata) (PC, 2).

....

EVANGELICAL COUNSELS AND THE COMMON LIFE (PC, 12–15)

Chastity, poverty and obedience each receive an article. Warmly affirming chastity "for the sake of the kingdom of heaven," PC does not say that the religious state is higher than marriage (but see OT, 10). The text challenges religious orders themselves (and not just their members) to give a kind of corporate witness to poverty. And obedience includes listening on the part of superiors. The article on common life calls on institutes to avoid unhealthy divisions with the community.

PARTICULAR ISSUES (PC, 16–25)

The first fifteen articles of PC were newly written after debate at the Council's third session in response to the bishops' many suggestions. The rest of the document (PC, 16–24) changed little from the earlier draft. These articles treat particular issues. Of these, one of the most visible reforms since the Council has been the simplifying of religious clothes (PC, 17). And one of the most important has been the attention given to the education of members of religious orders (PC, 18). A general exhortation concludes the document (PC, 25).

THE DOCUMENT TODAY

CHARISMS AND COUNSELS

Two themes are held in tension by PC. On the one hand, the text emphasizes the centrality of the evangelical counsels of chastity, poverty and obedience. This theme emphasizes the commonality among all religious institutes. On the other hand, the text emphasizes the distinctive charism, or vision, that each community can trace back to its founder. This theme emphasizes their differences.

SISTERS AND NUNS

If we think of hospitals and schools, orphanages and outreach, it is not an exaggeration to say that most of the ministry in the history of American Catholicism has been done by women. Religious sisters and nuns have supported some of the church's most important activities, from passing on the faith to caring for the needy. After the Council, their ministry continued, but in new forms. As these women embraced Vatican II's spirit of engagement with the world, they left support positions and parochial schools in order to minister in parishes or to live more closely with the poor. At the same time, larger historical shifts (particularly the opening up of new roles for women in society after the 1960s) marked the beginning of a decline in the number of religious. At the end of the Council, there were almost 180,000 sisters and nuns in the United States. Today, there are fewer than 70,000—and the high median age of these sisters means that many of them are no longer in active ministry. Communities of women religious today are caught between caring for their older members and searching for some way to hand on their mission.

....

Who Participates in a Council?

We usually speak of the *bishops* of Vatican II. But tradition and church law have allowed some non-bishops to attend councils and have a deliberate vote there. Included among the some twenty-eight hundred individuals summoned to Vatican II were about one hundred abbots and general superiors of men's religious orders and congregations. These non-bishops were full participants at the Council—serving on commissions, speaking in the council hall and voting on the documents. Unfortunately, the heads of women's religious orders were excluded.

....

FOR REFLECTION

- Read *PC*, 2, 12–14: Reflect on the distinctive spirituality of a religious order you know something about. What is attractive about the special vision of this order?

- Read *PC*, 1–2, 24–25: How are communities of women religious to hand on their mission? What might "adaptation to the changed conditions of our time" (*PC*, 2) mean for religious life today?

···

9

DECREE ON THE APOSTOLATE OF LAY PEOPLE
Apostolicam Actuositatem
The Decree on the Apostolate of Lay People *(AA)* is remarkable not so much for *what* it says, but *that* it says it at all. By placing the laity as a major issue on the agenda, Pope John XXIII set Vatican II apart from all previous councils.

CATHOLIC ACTION
The Catholic church witnessed a "rebirth of the laity" in the decades leading up to Vatican II. In the United States, groups like the Christian Family Movement, the Legion of Decency, and the National Councils of Catholic Men and Women were formed by laypeople intent on carrying forward the "apostolate," or mission, of the church. In Europe, groups like these were known as "Catholic Action."

Popes from Pius X (1903–1914) to Pius XII (1939–1958) encouraged Catholic Action. Pius XI (1922–1939), the movement's greatest proponent, defined it as "the participation of the laity in the apostolate of the Church's hierarchy." He saw Catholic Action as a powerful force for extending the church's influence into family, political life and the world of work. But some laity complained that Catholic Action was too rigid, monolithic and clergy-controlled. Usually, the hierarchy authorized these movements and closely supervised them—giving the impression that the laity were simply the "long arm of the hierarchy."

They appeared to "help out" with a mission that really belonged to the ordained.

EVERYONE IS AN APOSTLE

The Council's preparatory commission on the lay apostolate inherited these ambiguities. Everyone agreed on the need to affirm the laity's contribution to the church's mission. The question was how much autonomy should be allowed. Some wanted a top-down version of Catholic Action to be the model for all lay activity. Others wanted to encourage more independent forms of the lay apostolate. In the end, the document praised Catholic Action, but presented it as one among many ways in which laypeople can serve.

The debate surrounding Catholic Action—and the inordinate time *AA* spends on different forms of the apostolate—should not distract us from what is really revolutionary in the document, namely, the claim that Christ himself calls every baptized believer to serve the mission of the church (*AA,* 3). The apostolate does not belong to the hierarchy; it belongs to everyone. When Cardinal Fernando Cento presented this document to the assembly, he called this insight the heart of the text. He said that the deepest desire of the drafting commission was to help all the baptized see that no one can be a genuine Christian without also being an apostle. If this realization were achieved, he concluded, it would be the greatest triumph of the Second Vatican Council.

A THEME THROUGHOUT THE COUNCIL

After Cento's introduction, the bishops began debate (which ran October 6–13, 1964). Despite the document's affirmation of the laity, it still seemed to be a text written by clerics for clerics. Several speakers pointed this out. They also criticized the draft's lack of theological foundations and its poor arrangement. The commission for the lay apostolate had earlier resisted the coordinating commission's instruc-

> **❝** In the church, there is diversity of ministry but unity of mission **❞** (*AA*, 2).

tions to cut down their text to a few short propositions. Nevertheless, large chunks of material were siphoned off to be included in the documents on the church *(LG)* and the church in the modern world *(GS)*. For the theme of the laity ran throughout the whole council. The final version of *AA* addressed some of these concerns, at the same time citing several other council texts that treat the laity—the documents on church, liturgy, media, ecumenism, bishops and Christian education.

READING GUIDE

The Council turns to the laity in order to intensify the apostolic activity *(apostolicam actuositatem)* of the whole people of God. *AA* states that the activity of the laity was important at the very beginning of the church, and it remains so today.

CHAPTER ONE: THE VOCATION OF LAY PEOPLE TO THE APOSTOLATE (*AA*, 2–4)

One Mission, Many Ministries (*AA*, 2)

Chapter one lays out the theological foundations for the lay apostolate. Much of this chapter was rewritten after the Constitution on the Church *(LG)* was promulgated (November 21, 1964). It thus reflects *LG*'s positive vision.

The chapter begins with the mission of the whole church. This mission is twofold: the salvation of all people and the renewal of the world. Both aspects of this mission belong to everyone in the church—clergy and laity—by virtue of their membership in the body of Christ. In a living body, no member is passive.

....

Ministry or Apostolate?

Today we talk a lot about *lay ministry*. But that was not the case at Vatican II. In the language of the time, *ministry* was something the clergy did. The laity had an *apostolate*. After the Council, the language shifted so that what Vatican II meant by *lay apostolate* — namely, any activity by laypersons that serves the mission of the church (*AA*, 2)—is what we usually mean today when we speak of *lay ministry*.

....

The laity play their own role in this mission. They share in the prophetic, priestly and kingly work of Christ by evangelizing, sanctifying and witnessing to others. *AA* follows *LG,* 31, by describing the secular character of the laity. They live in the "midst of the world and of secular affairs." But their apostolate is not limited there. Indeed, the laity contribute to the mission of the whole people of God both *in the world* and *in the church.*

Christ and the Spirit (AA, 3)

The laity receive their share in the mission of the church directly from Christ himself. Their right and duty to be apostles comes from their union with Christ their head. This is the single most important insight of the document—overturning a hierarchical view in which all church activity trickles down through the clergy. Instead of this top-down vision the movement of the article is bottom-up. The Holy Spirit gives special gifts and charisms to the people of God. The pastors in turn judge these gifts, careful not to quench the Spirit, but to test everything and keep what is good.

A Lay Spirituality (AA, 4)

The success of the apostolate depends on the laity's living union with Christ. This relationship takes place in the context of each person's ordinary, daily life. A lay spirituality does not deny life in the world. Instead, it seeks to find God always and everywhere present.

CHAPTER TWO: OBJECTIVES (*AA,* 5–8)

The goals of the lay apostolate are the goals of the church: to bring all people to salvation and to renew the whole world. This twofold objective is confused by a threefold division of this chapter into spiritual activity, secular activity and charitable activity. (The arrangement goes back to the original division of the commission on the lay apostolate into three subcommittees: on Catholic Action, on social issues and on charitable works.) Just as the clergy minister to word and sacrament, the laity, in their own way, evangelize and sanctify others in and outside the church. Working to renew the secular world is the distinctive task of the laity, whose faith ought to permeate their families, workplaces and communities. Finally, the chapter recommends direct charitable assistance to the poor, sick and dispossessed.

CHAPTER THREE: VARIOUS FIELDS OF THE APOSTOLATE (*AA*, 9–14)

Chapter three highlights several realms in which the laity exercise their apostolate "both in the church and in the world" (*AA*, 9). A special mention of women is included here thanks to the suggestion of the women observers, who advised the commission during the Council's third and fourth sessions.

Laity are active in church communities through outreach, catechesis and administration. The drafters of these encouraging words could not have

Layman's Terms

The Council's commission for the lay apostolate—made up entirely of clergy—soon recognized the obvious: They needed advice from laypeople! But at the beginning of the Council, the rules did not allow for any formal lay participation. And so the first consultation took place in secret. When an international organization of lay leaders gathered in Rome in February of 1963, advisers to the commission "dropped in" on their meeting. By the fall things had changed. At the start of the Council's second session, Pope Paul VI announced that thirteen laymen would be invited as official observers. The number of lay observers would grow and eventually come to include women. One of these observers, Patrick Keegan (president of the International Catholic Worker's Movement), would address the whole assembly of bishops on the last day of debate on *AA*.

predicted the explosion of parish-based lay ministries that would follow the Council. The few church roles named here are only a glimmer of what was to come. Family and youth are important sources and arenas for the lay apostolate. And the chapter describes how the laity's responsibility to serve Christ extends from one's immediate surroundings (*AA*, 13) to the national and international levels (*AA*, 14).

CHAPTER FOUR: DIFFERENT FORMS OF THE APOSTOLATE (*AA*, 15–22)

AA is marked by a certain repetitiveness as the lay apostolate is considered from several different angles. An earlier draft of chapter four focused on different types of groups and associations (such as Catholic Action). But the bishops wanted to give greater attention to the ways in which individual laypeople serve the church's mission. So chapter four was divided into two parts: individual and group forms of apostolate. In the process, the individual apostolate was affirmed as the starting point and condition of all lay activity in the church (*AA*, 16). Catholic Action—which generated so much enthusiasm and debate prior to the Council—is recognized as one type of group apostolate (*AA*, 19–10).

CHAPTER FIVE: PRESERVING ORDER (*AA*, 23–27)

Chapter five makes the important point that the hierarchy holds the primary responsibility for coordinating activities within and on behalf of the church (*AA*, 23). But the detailed discussion of how the hierarchy relates to various forms of the apostolate (seen both here and in chapter four) reflects concerns that were important at the time. After the Council, as group apostolates became less important—especially in the United States—so did the distinctions outlined here. The chapter's call for establishing a Vatican office on the laity, however, did take concrete shape after the Council (*AA*, 26). And the call for Catholics to collaborate with non-Catholics was embraced (*AA*, 27).

CHAPTER SIX: TRAINING FOR THE APOSTOLATE (*AA*, 28–33)

A final chapter offers basic principles to guide the formation for the lay apostolate. Notable is its attention to the distinctive features of the layperson's life and its holistic approach.

THE DOCUMENT TODAY

LAY ECCLESIAL MINISTRY

After the Council, Catholic Action all but disappeared—and so did the language of "lay apostolate." In its place came "lay ministry." Inspired by the Council's vision and encouraged by their pastors, laywomen and laymen began to take up tasks traditionally reserved to priests or nuns: distributing Communion, reading at Mass, running parish programs in education and outreach. In the United States, parishes began to hire laypeople as religious education directors, liturgical coordinators and youth ministers. Not just an occasional volunteer opportunity, lay ministry became for many a career and a vocation.

The U.S. bishops have come to call this group of professionally prepared, full-time parish ministers "lay ecclesial ministers." There are currently more than thirty thousand lay ecclesial ministers working in parishes in the United States—more than the number of diocesan priests. With thousands more in lay ministry formation programs around the country, the growth of this new group of ministers shows no sign of slowing.

A Positive View of the Laity

In much of church law, the laity have been defined negatively—according to who they weren't (the clergy) or what they couldn't do (preach, lead, sanctify and so on). Bishop Stephen László of Austria brought this point home during debate on the lay apostolate. He described an old theological dictionary whose entry on the laity read simply: "Laity, see clergy." It offered no positive treatment. László argued that the proposed document was certainly an advance over this older view. But more needed to be done to say who the laity are, and not just who they aren't.

A SECULAR LAITY

By describing the laity as "secular," the bishops at Vatican II were not criticizing them (see *LG,* 31). Instead, they were trying to offer a positive description of the lay vocation. The laity live "in the world." This is where they do God's work. By taking their Christian faith into the marketplace, into their homes and families, into their work and politics, the laity serve to illuminate the world with the light of Christ. Their "secularity" is not a liability; it is a great opportunity.

Some complain that the laity have failed to embrace this call to transform the world. Too many laypeople continue to separate their religious faith from their daily lives. But others argue that this is the wrong way to frame the question. Talk of the laity's "secular vocation" is inadequate, for it is not just the laity who are "in the world," but the *whole church*. The responsibility to renew the secular sphere does not belong to the laity alone. It belongs to the entire people of God—clergy and laity. It is the *whole church* that is a leaven in the world, working to transform all of society into the family of God (see *GS,* 40). Laity and clergy may go about this work differently. But if we separate too rigidly clergy in the church from laity in the world, both groups suffer, as does the mission of the church.

THE CRITICAL FUNCTION OF LAY GROUPS

While the pre-conciliar model of Catholic Action may have faded, Catholic laity continue to form associations and groups. Some of these groups have challenged—to varying degrees—official church teaching and practice (for example, the Women's Ordination Conference, Call to Action, Voice of the Faithful). These groups see themselves as playing a critical function by calling the church to ongoing renewal and reform. Not surprisingly, they often encounter resistance from the hierarchy.

FOR REFLECTION
• Read *AA,* 2–3, 6, 22, 24: What are the theological themes of Vatican II that you see supporting the role of lay ecclesial ministry?
• Read *AA,* 2, 4, 7: What does it mean to "renew the temporal order" today? What aspects of the world today need transformation? How might a layperson work toward this transformation? How might an ordained person? How might you?

• Read *AA,* 23–25: What principles in *AA* do you find most helpful in understanding the relationship between the laity and the hierarchy? Is it ever appropriate to be critical of the church's positions? If so, what is appropriate disagreement and what is inappropriate?

....

10

DECREE ON ECUMENISM

Unitatis Redintegratio

Ecumenism is the search for unity among those Christian churches that sadly separated from one another over the course of history. Vatican II took up this theme in its Decree on Ecumenism *(UR)*. But the concern for Christian unity extended beyond this short document. It permeated the work of the whole Council.

BETTER LATE THAN NEVER

The twentieth century was the century of the ecumenical movement. This movement began among Protestants hoping to better coordinate their missionary work. It grew into a series of international gatherings that took up questions of doctrine as well as practice. The hope was that these meetings would help overcome denominational divisions. A milestone came in 1948, when representatives from 147 Protestant, Anglican and Orthodox churches established the World Council of Churches in order to provide a forum for ongoing conversation and to promote the work of Christian unity.

Early on, the Roman Catholic church distanced itself from these developments. Catholics were forbidden to take part in ecumenical gatherings. The Vatican argued that participation in such assemblies would falsely imply that one church is as valid as another. Pope Pius XI's 1928 encyclical *Mortalium Animos* set the tone by arguing that the only way to foster Christian unity is to encourage wayward heretics and schismatics to repent and come back to the one true church of Christ. Reunion meant *return* to the Roman Catholic church.

But things began to change in the 1950s. A letter from the Holy Office spoke of the ecumenical movement as inspired by the Holy Spirit. Catholic experts were allowed (under strict conditions) to participate in some dialogue. The real breakthrough came with the election of Pope John XXIII. His openness to other Christians and his repeated emphasis on unity alarmed his closest advisers. From the beginning, he saw the movement toward Christian unity as one of Vatican II's primary goals. He established a Vatican Secretariat for Christian Unity to help prepare for the Council. And he brushed aside precedent by inviting Protestants and Orthodox to Vatican II as official observers.

Decree on Ecumenism

Introduction

Chapter One: Catholic Principles on Ecumenism

Chapter Two: The Practice of Ecumenism

Chapter Three: Churches and Ecclesial Communities Separated From the Roman Apostolic See

TOO MANY COOKS

When Vatican II began, there were three different draft documents touching on ecumenism: (1) a document on Eastern Orthodoxy, written by the Commission for Eastern Churches, (2) a chapter on ecumenism in the church document, written by Cardinal Ottaviani's Theological Commission, and (3) a draft on general ecumenical principles, written by the Secretariat for Christian Unity, headed by Cardinal Bea.

The overlap was due in part to turf battles among the various commissions. Each argued that they alone had competence in this area. Ottaviani believed all doctrinal issues belonged to his commission. Bea, whose secretariat had just been elevated to the same level as the other council commissions, argued that he should coordinate all ecumenical issues.

Catholic Principles of Ecumenism

When debate began on *UR* at the Council's second session, the first chapter of the document was titled: "The Principles of Catholic Ecumenism." This title might have given the impression that there is more than one ecumenical movement, that the Roman Catholic church was setting up its own ecumenism alongside the ecumenism already underway among Protestants. Several bishops requested that the title be changed from "The Principles of Catholic Ecumenism" to "The Catholic Principles of Ecumenism" (which, in the Latin text, required only the addition of a single letter *s*). The new title better reflects the fact that there is only one movement toward Christian unity, which the Catholic church now joins.

In fact, only the first document—the draft on unity with the Orthodox—was debated at the first session of the Council. Few rejected the substance of the draft. But it was criticized for its authoritative tone. It seemed to lack a spirit of dialogue. Cardinal Liénart of France felt the draft's insistence on a "return" to the one true church was an insurmountable obstacle to ecumenism. Furthermore, Patriarch Maximos IV Sayegh (who represented the Melkite churches in union with Rome) accused the draft of a "Latin" bias. He pointed out that the Eastern churches—both those in union with Rome and those separated from Rome—have their own rites, traditions and organizational structures that ought to be respected. He joined several other bishops in asking that the three separate documents be combined into one. Quoting an old Arab proverb, the patriarch said, "When many hands prepare the cooking, the meat is sure to be burnt." At the end of debate, Cardinal Bea proposed that his secretariat be responsible for preparing a single document that would draw together the three drafts. The Council approved his recommendation, tactfully allowing for a thorough revision.

We Have Only Just Begun

By the start of the second session, a completely new draft on ecumenism was ready. It consisted of five chapters: (1) principles of Catholic ecumenism, (2) practical aspects of ecumenism, (3) Christian communities separated from the Catholic church, (4) non-Christians, especially Jews, and (5) religious liberty. For the purposes of debate, chapters four and five were immediately set aside. They had grown out of Bea's secretariat and had been attached here in order to ensure them a place on the agenda. Eventually, they would evolve into two separate documents (but only after a troubled and turbulent ride that lasted the length of the Council).

Debate thus began on the first three chapters, which were well received by the assembly. The new text offered a positive assessment of the ecumenical movement and demonstrated an openness to dialogue with other Christian churches. It presented ecumenism not as a perfect system, but as an open movement, the beginning of a process with the potential to lead the Christian churches in genuinely new directions. After further revision between the second and third sessions, the document was approved by an overwhelming vote (2,137 to 11) and formally promulgated on November 21, 1964.

❝ Before offering himself up as a spotless victim upon the altar of the cross, he prayed to his Father for those who believe: 'that all may be one, as you, Father, are in me, and I in you; I pray that they may be one in us, that the world may believe that you sent me' **❞** (*UR*, 2).

Reading Guide

The restoration of unity *(unitatis redintegratio)* among all Christians was one of the main concerns of Vatican II. *UR* takes up this concern directly by proposing guidelines to help Catholics work toward unity.

The document takes its point of departure from the concrete ecumenical movement already underway among various Christian communities (*UR*, 1). It encourages Catholics to join this movement

The Meaning of *Ecumenism*

The word *ecumenism* derives from the Greek word *oikumene*, which means "the whole world." Traditionally, Catholics have used the word to describe a general or universal council, one that represents the church of "the whole world" (Vatican II is counted as the twenty-first ecumenical council). But Protestants and other Christians adopted this word to describe those movements toward Christian unity that took place on a worldwide scale in the nineteenth and early twentieth centuries. As a result, the meaning of the word *ecumenism* itself changed, taking on the overtones of sympathy, openness and dialogue associated with this movement.

and offers some general principles (chapter one), practical suggestions (chapter two) and reflections on those Christian communities separated from the Catholic church (chapter three).

CHAPTER ONE: CATHOLIC PRINCIPLES OF ECUMENISM (*UR*, 2–4)

The Trinity, Source of Church Unity (UR, 2)

Chapter one begins with Christ's prayer that all believers may be one as he and the Father are one (John 17:21). It describes the Holy Spirit holding together all of the faithful in union with Christ. Indeed, the example and source of the unity of the church is the unity of Father, Son and Holy Spirit. In addition to this invisible source of unity in the Trinity, the text also names those visible elements of unity found in the Catholic church: confession of one faith, common worship and institutional unity— all guaranteed by the successors of Peter and the apostles, the pope and bishops. Here we see *UR*'s method. In encouraging openness and dialogue with others, the text does not hesitate to make clear the Catholic church's own self-understanding.

Restoration, Not Return (UR, 3)

After noting the ideal of unity in article 2, article 3 turns to the reality of disunity. In a remarkable admission, *UR* states that people on both sides were to blame for the historical splits that fractured Christianity. No one today can be blamed for these past divisions. Indeed, separated Christians are to be seen as brothers and sisters in Christ.

Following the Constitution on the Church (*LG,* 8, 15), *UR* drops the language of church membership, and with it the distracting question of who is and who is not "in" the church. Instead, *UR* speaks of degrees of communion among Catholics and other Christians.

The decree does not just speak about individuals, it affirms the value of other Christian churches and communities as such. There are elements of what it takes to constitute a "church" that exist outside of the Catholic church: Scripture, baptism, the life of grace, faith, hope, charity, the gifts of the Spirit, even certain church institutions. Other communities may lack some of the structures that Catholics see as essential to being a church (such as the apostolic succession of bishops or a valid Eucharist), but God nonetheless works through these communities to bring their members to salvation. Non-Catholic Christians are brought to salvation not *despite* their churches, but *because* of them.

In all of this, *UR* does not abandon the Catholic belief that only the Catholic church contains "the fullness of the means of salvation" (*UR,* 3). But no longer is ecumenism envisioned as a process in which the Catholic church simply waits for non-Catholics to *return* to it. Instead, ecumenism becomes a task of *restoring* unity, a unity that all churches—including the Catholic church—have to work toward.

The Little Things

Two days after the opening of the Second Vatican Council, Pope John XXIII met with the non-Catholic observers who had been formally invited to participate at the Council. Instead of sitting on the papal throne as was customary, Pope John used a chair similar to those used by the observers, and he sat at their level. This small symbolic gesture of equality was not lost on those in attendance.

Excommunications Lifted

At the last public session of the Second Vatican Council (December 7, 1965), a joint declaration of Pope Paul VI and the Orthodox Patriarch Athenagoras I was read out to the assembly. Together these leaders expressed regret for the offensive words, distrust and despicable acts that had poisoned the relationship between their churches for over a thousand years. They lifted the mutual excommunications of the eleventh century that had symbolically marked the split between East and West. And they expressed hope for future reconciliation.

Steps Toward Unity (UR, 4)

All Catholics are to participate, in some way, in the ecumenical movement. This movement proceeds in a series of steps: (1) avoiding negative stereotypes or false assumptions about other Christians, (2) dialogue between experts from different churches, (3) joint projects or initiatives that serve the needy, (4) common prayer when appropriate, and (5) self-reform and renewal. Participating in ecumenism demands that the Catholic church get its own household in order. Genuine reform and renewal is necessary to move forward toward Christian unity.

CHAPTER TWO: THE PRACTICE OF ECUMENISM *(UR, 5–12)*

Praying Together (UR, 5–8)

After discussing the ecumenical significance of reform and renewal within the Catholic church *(UR, 6)*, chapter two states that true ecumenism begins with an interior conversion, a willingness to ask pardon and offer forgiveness. At times, praying together with other Christians is not only possible, but desirable. However, common worship is not to be used indiscriminately as a way to restore unity among Christians. Held in tension here is the church's twofold conviction that the Eucharist is both sign and cause of church unity. As sign, common worship is generally forbidden—for the Eucharist cannot symbolize a unity that does not exist. As cause, common worship is sometimes commended—for in worshiping together we allow God's grace to lead us toward unity.

Learning Together (UR, 9–11)

Catholics should learn more about the beliefs and practices of other Christians. This is done best in meetings of the two sides where discussion can take place on an equal footing (*UR,* 9). Theology should be taught with an ecumenical sensitivity (*UR,* 10). And in ecumenical dialogue, all should keep in mind that in Catholic doctrine there exists a hierarchy of truths (*UR,* 11). Not everything the church teaches is equally central to the faith. And dialogue should not become so obsessed with differences over secondary matters that the more primary agreement on fundamental truths of the faith is overlooked.

Working Together (UR, 12)

Cooperation among Christian churches on common causes that help make the world a better place is one of the best ways to develop mutual understanding and to pave the road toward Christian unity.

CHAPTER THREE: CHURCHES AND ECCLESIAL COMMUNITIES SEPARATED FROM ROME (*UR,* 13–24)

Chapter three describes the two main groups of communities with which the Catholic church hopes to dialogue. For historical, political and theological reasons the churches of the East (Orthodox) and the churches and communities of the West (Protestant, Anglican) are quite distinct and thus raise different issues for ecumenical dialogue.

Churches of the East (UR, 14–18)

UR notes the ways in which the Roman Catholic church is indebted to the East. The great Greek-speaking theologians of the early church and the first doctrinal councils articulated the beliefs and creeds still cherished by most Christians today (*UR,* 14). Moreover, the Eastern churches (commonly called Orthodox) have a special relationship with the Catholic church. For although these churches are separated from Rome, they share with the Roman church most of the essential elements of church structure, belief and worship. They have maintained the apostolic succession of bishops and valid sacraments. Thus common worship is more easily encouraged (*UR*, 15). *UR* recognizes that the diverse disciplines, customs and liturgical practices of the East do not threaten the unity of the church, but add to its beauty (*UR*, 16). In fact, those Eastern Catholic churches that have maintained communion with Rome are an example of the legitimate diversity that is possible (*UR*, 17).

Churches and Communities of the West (*UR*, 19–24)

Those churches and ecclesial communities that emerged in the West out of the sixteenth-century Reformation pose a more difficult challenge for Catholics. Not only are these communities much more numerous and diverse than the Orthodox, but they often hold doctrines that differ significantly from those of the Catholic church. Acknowledging these difficulties, *UR* begins with what is held in common: confession of Jesus Christ as Lord and Savior, Scripture, baptism and worship, the effort to live a Christian moral life. In this, *UR* is not afraid of pointing out differences (such as the way in which Scripture is interpreted or differing understandings of the Eucharist), but overall the document offers a positive view of the possibility of dialogue.

The decree ends with a look to the future, recognizing that the reconciliation of all Christians is beyond human effort alone. Instead, *UR* places its hope in Christ's prayer of unity for his church (*UR*, 24).

THE DOCUMENT TODAY

THE FULLNESS OF THE MEANS OF SALVATION

What was striking about *UR* in 1964 was its openness. At a time when Catholics were taught to question the very possibility of salvation for Protestants, the document's affirmation of the salvific value of other churches was a real breakthrough. But today, *UR*'s claim that the Catholic church alone possesses the "fullness of the means of salvation" might seem arrogant and patronizing. Here it is important to remember the distinction between abstract essentials and the way in which these essentials are actually lived out. *UR* is not saying that

Catholics have a fuller salvation—that they are somehow "more" saved than Protestants. Rather, it is saying that the Catholic church has within it all the institutional *means* to help its members toward salvation. As one commentator put it, the Catholic church has a complete set of tools—the creed, a ministry linked to the apostles through apostolic succession and all seven sacraments. But the fact that the Catholic church has all the abstract essentials does not deny that many Protestants might actually be doing better in practice. Protestant churches can do an excellent job with the tools they have. And while the Catholic church affirms that structures and beliefs are important, it also recognizes that what is ultimately important is what these structures and beliefs serve: salvation itself. In the end, it's not the number of tools in your toolbox that matters, but the finished product those tools have helped create.

INTERCOMMUNION

Intercommunion is the sharing in liturgical worship, especially the Eucharist, between separated Christians (also known as "eucharistic sharing" or "eucharistic hospitality"). *UR* opened the door to intercommunion for Catholics, who until Vatican II had been strictly prohibited from it. But the document warned that worship in common should not be used indiscriminately for the restoration of Christian unity. Two principles must be maintained: (1) common worship presupposes common faith, and (2) sacraments are sources of grace. Because the churches remain divided in faith, intercommunion is ordinarily prohibited. But because the Eucharist is a source of grace, the sharing of Eucharist is possible and even necessary in certain circumstances.

Since Vatican II many ecumenically minded theologians have called for greater eucharistic sharing in order to promote the movement of churches toward unity (emphasizing the Eucharist as a *source* of unity). Rome however maintains that not enough ecumenical agreement has been achieved among churches to warrant full intercommunion (emphasizing the Eucharist as a *sign* of unity). The 1983 Code of

Canon Law prohibits eucharistic sharing between Catholic and non-Catholic Christians in general, but it allows for several important exceptions (see canon 844). When necessary, Catholics who do not have access to a Catholic priest may receive penance, Eucharist and anointing of the sick "from non-Catholic ministers in whose churches these sacraments are valid" (this applies most clearly to receiving sacraments in the Eastern Orthodox churches). Also, Catholic ministers may offer these same sacraments to non-Catholic Christians if these other Christians do not have access to their own ministers, if there is a serious spiritual need, if they ask for the sacrament on their own, if they share Catholic belief about the sacrament and if they are properly disposed.

ECUMENISM AT THE LOCAL LEVEL

Recent decades have seen enormous progress in ecumenical dialogue at the national and international levels. Theologians and officials from various churches have engaged in multi-year studies of various theological and historical questions. These dialogues have produced dozens of important documents and common statements—including the 1997 *Joint Declaration on the Doctrine of Justification,* cosigned by representatives from the Vatican and the Lutheran World Federation, a document that expresses agreement on some of the most divisive issues of the Protestant Reformation. But in many ways the "ecumenical movement" has been carried forward by a small group of experts and concerned Christians. What about the average Catholic? Have we taken seriously *UR*'s call for *everyone* in the church to work for Christian unity?

FOR REFLECTION

• Read *UR,* 3: Do you find the language of the "fullness of the means of salvation" helpful or unhelpful? What are some objections that might be raised? Are there other ways to say what *UR* is trying to say here?

- Read *UR,* 8: Should there be more or less eucharistic sharing among Christian churches? Why? Describe a worship experience you have had in a Christian tradition other than your own. Did you feel welcomed? Reflect on the Catholic Mass. In what ways is it welcoming to non-Catholics? In what ways is it not welcoming?
- Read *UR,* 5–7: Do you see a concern for ecumenism alive in your own parish or community? Give examples. What are some ways that "people in the pews" can contribute to the movement toward Christian unity?

DECREE ON THE CATHOLIC EASTERN CHURCHES
Orientalium Ecclesiarum

Within Catholicism there exists a number of churches that celebrate their own distinctive liturgy, practice their own customs and maintain their own organizational structure. These churches can look very much like Eastern Orthodox churches—their rites are elaborate and ornate, their hierarchies include patriarchs and married priests. But these are not Eastern Orthodox churches. They are Eastern *Catholic* churches. Though they are not of the Roman Rite, they live in full union with Rome.

The history of these Catholic Eastern churches is complicated and contested (some churches trace their independent existence back to the beginning of Christianity, others formed later as part of a questionable attempt by Rome to win over converts from Orthodoxy). But today these non-Latin churches—the Armenian and Byzantine, Coptic and Chaldean, Maronite, Melkite and many others—stand as an example of the diversity possible within Catholicism. They are witnesses to the fact that the Catholic church is bigger than the *Roman* Catholic church.

The Decree on Catholic Eastern Churches *(OE)* grew out of Vatican II's preparatory commission on Eastern churches. Before the Council began, this commission drafted two sets of texts: one on the Eastern Orthodox, another on Eastern Catholics. Eventually, the material on the Orthodox was included in the Decree on Ecumenism, which dealt with all churches separated from Rome. The material on Eastern Catholic developed into a short decree of its own.

When *OE* finally came up for debate at the Council's third session, several bishops criticized its "Latinizing" tendencies. For centuries Rome had tried to compel the Catholic Eastern churches to adopt certain practices and church structures found in the Latin West. Critics complained that *OE* had not freed itself from this mentality, but others praised the progress that had been made. A study of the revisions made to *OE* over the course of the Council reveals a growing appreciation for the distinctive features of the Catholic Eastern churches. The decree was officially approved at the end of the third session, November 21, 1964.

....

Decree on the Catholic Eastern Churches

This document is not divided into chapters, but contains thirty articles.

....

READING GUIDE

The document begins with a clear affirmation of the Eastern churches *(Orientalium ecclesiarum)* and the part they play in the one undivided heritage of the universal church. But if the Catholic Eastern churches are truly part of the one Catholic church, then why this separate document? Aren't these churches—by definition—already included wherever the Council texts speak of the Catholic church? (*LG,* 13 and 23 mention the Catholic Eastern churches explicitly.)

During debate, some bishops complained that the very existence of a separate document was itself a sign of condescension, a patronizing gesture toward an overlooked stepchild. Others argued that the churches of the East, though fully Catholic, present a unique set of challenges and opportunities. Their distinctive identity had been for so long marginalized that it was appropriate to recognize their full and equal place (*OE,* 3) within the family.

....

African Drums Boom

Vatican II's daily meetings began with Mass. And each day Mass was celebrated in a different liturgical rite, which rotated over the length of the Council. For many bishops, this was their first encounter with the various liturgical traditions of the Catholic Eastern churches. It was a surprising glimpse of diversity in a church so dominated by the monolithic Latin liturgy. During the Council's first session, the African chanting and deep rhythms of the Ethiopian rite (celebrated by Archbishop Yemmeru Asrate of Addis Ababa on November 28, 1962) earned the astonished headline: "African drums boom in Vatican rite."

....

CATHOLIC EASTERN CHURCHES
(*OE*, 2–6)

For *OE,* these communities of Eastern Catholics are not just different *rites,* but distinct *churches* (*OE,* 2). The broader language is significant. It is not just liturgical differences that mark these communities. They stand as integral churches with their own hierarchies, disciplinary regulations and methods of governance. As such, they "have the right and duty to govern themselves according to their own special disciplines" (*OE,* 5). *OE* wishes to see the distinctive traditions of the Catholic Eastern churches preserved "whole and entire" (*OE,* 2).

PARTICULAR TRADITIONS AND PRACTICES
(*OE*, 7–29)

In moving to particulars, *OE*'s general affirmation becomes qualified. Here we see that the document—despite its positive statements—remains basically a Western text about the East. Many of these articles treat technical matters of canon law. The text lists certain rights of the Eastern patriarchs (bishops who preside over autonomous federations of dioceses, called patriarchates) and their synods, but it also recognizes the power of the pope to intervene (a sticking point for the patriarchs). Greater flexibility is seen in sacramental and liturgical practice. *OE* recognizes the Eastern practice of priests administering confirmation (*OE*, 13–14). It allows the Eastern custom of fulfilling one's Sunday obligation by participating in the Liturgy of the Hours (*OE*, 15). It calls for the restoration of the permanent diaconate in the East (*OE*, 17). But the text is silent on the Eastern practice of allowing married priests. Finally, a section reflecting on the relationship between the Catholic Eastern churches and the Eastern Orthodox churches includes general principles to guide common worship and shared communion among members of these churches (*OE*, 26–29).

CONCLUSION (*OE*, 30)

The text ends with special reference to the separated churches of the East, urging Christians everywhere to pray as Jesus did that "all may be one."

THE DOCUMENT TODAY

UNITY AND DIVERSITY

The existence of the Catholic Eastern churches reveals how unity can be maintained amidst tremendous diversity. These churches remind us that many of the things Catholics in the West think of as "essential" (such as a

> **❝** Between those churches there is such a wonderful communion that this variety, so far from diminishing the church's unity, rather serves to emphasize it **❞** (*OE*, 2).

The Language of the Universal Church

The Melkite Patriarch Maximus IV Sayegh—one of the most colorful figures of Vatican II—refused to deliver his council speeches in Latin. Latin was the language of the *Roman* Catholic church, he granted, but it was not the language of the *Catholic church*. The Catholic church includes an array of Eastern churches that have never used Latin in their official documents or liturgical life. To demand that all Catholics speak Latin is to presume that the Latin church speaks for all Catholics. Patriarch Maximus spoke French instead.

celibate clergy, certain sacramental practices or structures of governance) are not in fact essential. The absence of these features of church life (or their presence in very different forms) does not put the Eastern churches outside the fold of the one Catholic church.

FOR REFLECTION

• Read *OE*, 1–2: What implications does *OE*'s recognition of unity amid diversity have for the ecumenical movement, particularly with relations between Catholics and Orthodox? What implications does this have for diversity within the Roman Catholic church?

PART THREE

....

THE CHURCH IN THE WORLD

DECREE ON THE MASS MEDIA
Inter Mirifica

The Decree on the Mass Media *(IM)* was briefly debated at the Council's first session and quickly approved at the second. The speed with which the Council treated this text had little to do with the urgency of the topic. In fact, most of the bishops simply wanted to get it out of the way so that they could move on to what they considered more important issues. The result is a text generally considered to be one of the weakest of the Council.

During the first half of the twentieth century, the church responded cautiously to the rise of the modern media. This caution is captured well by the title of Pope Pius XI's 1936 encyclical on motion pictures, *Vigilanti Cura* (With a Watchful Eye). A more positive approach emerged under Pope Pius XII. His 1957 encyclical on film, radio and television, *Miranda Prorsus* (Very Remarkable Inventions), shows an appreciation for the opportunities afforded by these new technologies.

Vatican II's *IM* tries to follow Pius XII's more positive approach. It affirms the value of the modern media, but its tone is paternalistic and moralizing. And because it was dispatched so early in the Council, the document remains relatively untouched by many of the themes that came to define Vatican II. It provides no real ecclesiological foundation for its specific exhortations. It offers little reflection on the role of the

Decree on the Mass Media

This document contains two untitled chapters and a conclusion.

laity in the media or the impact of ecumenism on these questions. These limitations are themselves a testimony to how far the Council advanced over the course of its four sessions. But they hold back the document itself, which opens a door but does not go through it.

READING GUIDE

IM locates the modern media among the marvelous *(inter mirifica)* inventions human beings have produced with the help of God. Following a recognition of the benefits of the media (the press, cinema, radio, television and the like) comes a warning about its damaging potential (*IM*, 2). Throughout the document we see this affirmation of the proper use of the media alongside a condemnation of its misuse.

CHAPTER ONE (*IM*, 3–12)

The first chapter insists that all aspects of the media must be used morally. This applies to those who watch, read or listen to the media (*IM*, 9), especially children (*IM*, 10), as well as those who produce various media (*IM*, 11) and those who regulate it (*IM*, 12). All should base their choices and decisions on sound moral principles.

CHAPTER TWO (*IM*, 13–24)

The second chapter addresses how the church itself uses the media in fulfilling its mission. It calls for the support of a Catholic press and the production of good, moral films and programs (*IM*, 14, 17). Great emphasis is placed on the education of priests, religious and laity involved in producing these programs and publications (*IM*, 15), as well as formation for those who use them (*IM*, 16). Diocesan, national and international initiatives are encouraged (*IM*, 18–22). *IM* then concludes with a specific request for a follow-up document (*IM*, 23). The result was the 1971 Pastoral Instruction on the Means of Social Communication *(Communio et Progressio),* a longer, more constructive and more open document.

THE DOCUMENT TODAY

COMMUNICATION WITHIN THE CHURCH

Communio et Progressio states: "Since the development of public opinion within the church is essential, individual Catholics have the right to all the information they need to play their active role in the life of the church.... The normal flow of life and the smooth functioning of government within the church require a steady two-way flow of information."

> **"** All the members of the church should make a concerted effort to ensure that the media are utilized in the service of the many works of the apostolate without delay and as energetically as possible, where and when they are needed **"** (*IM*, 13).

THE IMPACT OF THE MEDIA

IM is marked by an instrumental view of the media. That is, it presents the media as a "means" that can be put to any end. It is a tool that can be used for good or for ill. But the assumption is that the tool itself is neutral.

More recently, theologians (and some church documents) have called into question this assumption of neutrality. Here they are not talking about biased broadcasters or slanted coverage of church events. The issue is deeper. These theologians argue that the pervasiveness of technology in the developed world and our total immersion in the virtual "alternative universe" of television, Internet and advertising has shaped the very way in which we relate to the real world. It is not just *what* we watch on television, but *how* we watch it that influences us. Television and other technologies have trained us to a certain way of responding to everything else in our lives—including our religious faith. Thus the minimal demands that television makes on the viewer transforms us into passive "viewers" at church. The inescapable din of advertising trains us to treat the sacraments like consumer goods. The overwhelming amount of choice made possible by the Internet leads us to expect a variety of options in the moral sphere. The individualism reinforced through personal digital assistants and other technologies can weaken our appreciation for church community.

....

The Press at the Council

At first, the world press had difficulty getting information about what was happening at Vatican II. Though over a thousand press passes were issued for the Council's first session, the rules banned reporters from the council hall and bound all the bishops to secrecy. Those in charge seemed determined to control the flow of information. They argued that secrecy was necessary to protect the bishops' freedom to speak their minds (without having to worry about how it would appear in the papers the next day).

But the arrangement proved impossible. The reporters demanded hard news. To provide some response, the U.S. bishops established their own press panel, where every day a dozen or so American experts discussed the council debates with journalists. By the Council's second session, the official Vatican press releases became more substantive. But one of the earliest glimpses into the inner workings of the Council was a series of anonymous articles appearing in *The New Yorker*, signed by a mysterious figure, Xavier Rynne. Rynne—who years later identified himself as Francis X. Murphy, a Redemptorist priest teaching in Rome at the time of the Council—summarized the bishops' debates in a lively way, introducing American readers to the personalities and political maneuvering behind the Council.

....

For Reflection

• Read *IM,* 5: Is there freedom of information within the church? In what ways does the church and its leadership communicate well? In what areas is improvement needed?

• Read *IM,* 1–2: Can you think of any habits of action or thought in your own life that have been shaped by modern media? Are there positive as well as negative influences at work here? What is the role of the church in addressing these issues?

13

....

Decree on the Church's Missionary Activity
Ad Gentes

The Decree on the Church's Missionary Activity *(AG)* was promoted by missionaries and clergy from the Third World who wanted to generate support for their work of spreading the gospel. But they came face-to-face with others who saw the document as an opportunity to rethink the church's whole approach to evangelization. The result was a kind of compromise. The text affirms the work of the *missions* by placing this work in the context of the church's larger *mission*.

An Identity Crisis

At the time of the Council, almost everyone recognized that the church's missionary activity was facing an identity crisis. New attitudes were raising new questions. Was the church's approach too Western? Too tied to European models and expectations? Too patronizing toward the developing world? How successful had the church been in allowing the faith to really take root among native peoples and native cultures? In the face of widespread and systemic poverty, should the emphasis be on evangelization? Or should missionaries focus on socioeconomic development? What impact would the decline in vocations to the priesthood—already beginning to be felt—have on the church's missionary effort? And given the growing respect for freedom of conscience and an increasingly positive appreciation for other religions, was missionary activity even relevant anymore?

DRY BONES

By the time the Council assembly got around to debating missions, the prepared text had been reduced to thirteen short propositions. Several other documents had suffered a similar fate, part of an effort to speed up debate and bring the Council to a quick end. But there was widespread dissatisfaction with the short text. Most bishops felt that such an important topic deserved a fuller treatment. And so, many were surprised when Pope Paul VI visited the council assembly on the first day of debate in order to *endorse* the text. His praise of the draft seemed ill-advised. Three days later the assembly voted to reject these "dry bones," sending the document back to committee to be rewritten.

THE CHURCH'S MISSION AND THE MISSIONS

A new text was prepared by a small committee of bishops and theologians in the early months of 1965. Debate centered on whether the text should maintain the traditional notion of mission, namely, preaching the gospel to unbelievers and spreading the church into new lands, or whether it should speak of mission in a broader sense. Proponents of the latter view wanted to describe mission as the evangelization that shapes *all* aspects of the church's activity—even if this evangelization occurs among people who are already Christian. This broader understanding emerged out of efforts prior to the Council to respond to increased secularization in Europe, where even France—that "eldest daughter of the church"—was christened "missionary territory."

In the end, the commission chose to focus on the traditional under-standing of missionary activity, conceived as "preaching the gospel and implanting the church among people who do not yet believe in Christ" (*AG,* 6). Yet the missions are placed within the context of the activity of the whole church, which "is by its very nature missionary" (*AG,* 2). The most original contribution of the final draft is its theological intro-duction, which locates the church's mission within the trinitarian mis-sions of the Son and the Spirit, sent forth from the Father. This docu-ment was approved and promulgated at the end of the fourth session, December 7, 1965.

READING GUIDE

God has sent the church to the nations *(ad gentes)* to preach the gospel to all. This responsibility falls on the successors to the apostles and indeed on the whole people of God. The text of *AG* that we have today was written almost in its entirety in 1965, the final year of the Council. Therefore, more than any other decree or declaration, it benefits from the vision articulated in the earlier constitutions on the church *(LG)* and the church in the modern world *(GS)*. We see this in *AG*'s Introduction, which calls the church "the universal sacrament of salvation" and the "people of God."

CHAPTER ONE: DOCTRINAL PRINCIPLES (*AG,* 2–9)
The Missions of the Trinity (*AG,* 2–4)
Chapter one lays out the theological foundations for the church's missionary activity. As such, it differs significantly from the more practical suggestions of the following chapters. Chapter one was added to the document after a majority of bishops complained that an earlier draft lacked doctrinal depth.

The chapter begins with three articles on the Father, Son and Holy Spirit. It takes the central mystery of Christianity, the Trinity, as the foundation for all missionary activity. The Father is the loving source of the missions of the Son and the Spirit (*AG,* 2). The Son becomes

Preaching and Church-Planting

In trying to define missionary activity, the drafting commission faced two opposing schools of thought. On the one hand were those (influenced by Protestant approaches) who defined missionary activity as the proclamation of the gospel aimed at winning individual conversions. This approach was personal and Christ-centered. On the other hand were those (influenced by canon law) who defined missionary activity as the establishment of churches with a clergy that would provide sacraments and instruction for native peoples. This approach was more institutional, territorial and church-centered. Rather than settle this dispute, AG incorporated both approaches, defining missionary activity as both preaching and church-planting.

human in order to offer salvation; he commissions his followers to proclaim his saving message to all (*AG,* 3). The Spirit moves over the disciples at Pentecost, formally inaugurating the church's mission to the nations (*AG,* 4). Missionary activity is presented as one dynamic movement of "sending forth" that begins with the Father and extends through Christ, Spirit and church to the ends of the earth.

Mission and Missions (AG, 5–6)

Chapter one then describes the church's mission in its broadest sense as every activity of the church that serves to lead people to the faith, freedom and peace of Christ (*AG,* 5). It goes on to define one aspect of this broad mission, the aspect that is in fact the subject of the entire decree: the preaching of the gospel and implanting of the church among people who do not yet know Christ, namely, "the missions" (*AG,* 6). The text is careful to say that missionary activity is not the same thing as pastoral care of the faithful, nor the same as ecumenical outreach—however much these three are related.

The Importance of Missionary Activity (AG, 7–9)

Chapter one ends with a clear affirmation of the necessity and urgency of missionary activity (*AG,* 7), which fosters the true fulfillment of

human nature (*AG,* 8), and leads ultimately to the realization of God's plan
at the end of time (*AG,* 9).

CHAPTER TWO: MISSIONARY WORK (*AG,*
10–18)
Chapter two begins to take up some of
the practical steps necessary to accomplish the church's missionary task. This
work begins—for everyone in the
church—with living a genuine Christian life (*AG,* 11). In the missions, this
Christian witness takes shape through love that does not discriminate,
and it extends to include efforts to improve social and economic conditions, to seek justice and to promote human dignity (*AG,* 12). Preaching leads to conversion. And this conversion is assisted by a robust
process of Christian initiation (*AG,* 14). Finally, the formation of community ought to draw on the riches of the particular people and cultures
of a place. Special attention is given to catechists, those local laymen
and laywomen who lead the many small communities in missionary
territories where clergy are absent. These lay leaders are to be trained,
financially supported when appropriate, and recognized in a public
liturgical celebration (*AG,* 17).

CHAPTER THREE: PARTICULAR CHURCHES (*AG,* 19–22)
Chapter three considers missionary communities that have attained a
kind of stability and permanence. It calls on local churches around the
world to help support these "young churches," but it also calls on the
young churches to recognize their links with the universal church. This
is not always a relationship of dependency. For the young churches are
to be active agents themselves, reaching out to evangelize in their own
areas and even, when they are able, sending missionaries to other parts
of the world (*AG,* 20). A long article on the laity was added here (*AG,*

> **"** The church on earth is by
> its very nature missionary since,
> according to the plan of the
> Father, it has its origin in the
> mission of the Son and the holy
> Spirit **"** (AG, 2).

21, see also *AG*, 41) to respond to earlier complaints that the document presented a very hierarchical understanding of missionary activity.

Running throughout this chapter (and the document as a whole) is a thoroughly incarnational vision of the missions. The church should not impose an alien culture on native peoples. Just as Christ took up and transformed human flesh, the church must take up and transform those customs, traditions, teachings and other cultural dimensions of the people to whom it preaches (*AG*, 22).

CHAPTER FOUR: MISSIONARIES (*AG*, 23–27)

After reminding the reader that the responsibility to spread the faith belongs to every disciple of Christ, chapter four focuses on those who hear a special call to serve as missionaries. The chapter encourages these missionaries, describes the personal qualities needed to fulfill this task and addresses the need for appropriate formation.

CHAPTER FIVE: ORGANIZATION OF MISSIONARY ACTIVITY (*AG*, 28–34)

The most controversial issue of chapter five had to do with the role of the Vatican office for missions, the Congregation for the Propagation of the Faith *(Propaganda Fide)*. At the Council, many bishops from missionary areas accused the *Propaganda Fide* of relying on outdated methods, of being disconnected from the reality "on the ground" and of wielding power in what seemed to be an arbitrary way. The final text reaffirms the need for a single office to coordinate all missionary activity, but it encourages several reforms, including giving representatives of missionaries an active role and a deliberative vote in the decision-making process of the congregation (*AG*, 29).

CHAPTER SIX: COOPERATION (*AG*, 35–42)

The final chapter concludes by suggesting ways in which Catholics who do not live in mission territories can contribute to the church's missionary enterprise. The chapter's basic premise, repeating what has been said earlier, is that every member of the body of Christ has an obligation to help this body grow. Spreading the faith begins with interior conversion (*AG*, 35), and its most fundamental realization is the effort to lead a profound Christian life (*AG*, 36). Individuals and church communities themselves have a responsibility here (*AG*, 37). Bishops (*AG*, 38), priests (*AG*, 39), religious (*AG*, 40) and laity (*AG*, 41) all play a role. A greeting to missionaries and a prayer for them conclude the document (*AG*, 42).

THE DOCUMENT TODAY

FROM THE MISSIONS TO A NEW EVANGELIZATION

Following Vatican II, the older paradigm of missionary work that saw the European church "sending" and the rest of the world "receiving" gave way to a new paradigm: a vision of the whole worldwide church sharing together in the one mission of evangelizing the world. While in many ways *AG* was shaped by the concerns of the first paradigm, it anticipates the second.

This new paradigm is captured well by the phrase "new evangelization," which was first used by the bishops of Latin America gathered at Medellín in 1968. It was lifted up by Pope John Paul II to become a hallmark of his papacy.

What makes the new evangelization "new" is not the message—the good news of Jesus Christ remains the same always. Rather, it is new in approach, attitude and scope. It is an evangelization directed not to an unknown unbeliever in an unfamiliar corner of the world. Instead it is an evangelization directed to the whole world, its many cultures and its peoples, both those who have never heard of Christ and those who have heard the good news but forgotten what it means to follow Christ. The new evangelization includes not only initial proclamation and pastoral care, but also re-evangelization of those whose lives are no longer inspired by the gospel. Alongside preaching, the new evangelization demands dialogue (with other Christians, other religions and with all of humanity). And it requires serious attention to full human development—freedom from poverty, violence and unjust structures of oppression. The new evangelization employs the best of modern media, while respecting the dignity and freedom of those who listen and respond. And it calls everyone in the church, especially the laity, to participate in spreading the message of Christ.

....

The Pope Makes an Appearance

Pope Paul VI's appearance in St. Peter's Basilica on November 6, 1964, to endorse the document on missions was the only time either he or John XXIII attended a working session of Vatican II. According to canon law, the pope is the head of an ecumenical council. But since the Middle Ages, popes have chosen to absent themselves from daily meetings—wanting to avoid giving the impression that they were interfering with the freedom of debate. Why Paul VI chose to attend this session is unclear. Some interpreted it as a personal favor to Cardinal Gregorio Agagianian, who headed the commission on missionary activity. Others thought that the pope simply wanted to go on record as participating in this formal way—either as an expression of collegiality with his brother bishops or as a reminder of his leadership over them—and the decree on missions seemed the least controversial topic to do so. Unfortunately, because so many bishops were dissatisfied with the draft that the pope endorsed, his gesture ended up creating controversy itself.

....

FOR REFLECTION

• Read *AG,* 5: Which aspects of the new evangelization (proclamation, dialogue, work for social justice, responding to culture, use of media, respecting the freedom of individuals, involving the laity) do you see as most important? Why? Has the church been successful in embracing this new evangelization? What else needs to be done?

....

14

DECLARATION ON CHRISTIAN EDUCATION

Gravissimum Educationis

Over the course of the Council, this document evolved from a large and detailed draft called "On Catholic Schools" to a short statement of general principles, titled "Declaration on Christian Education" *(GE).* The change in title reflects a change in emphasis. Rather than locate education entirely within the Catholic school system, the Council chose to place the Catholic school system within a broader educational context.

When asked prior to the Council what topics Vatican II should consider, many bishops identified Catholic schools as a top priority. Their interest came for a variety of reasons. For one thing, in countries like the United States, the Catholic school system was huge—extensive and expensive. The very size of the system demanded a lot of attention from the bishops. At the same time, questions were beginning to be raised. What was being done for the many Catholic children *not* in these schools? How should the church respond to the monopolization of education by the state and the lack of financial support? What about the perception in parts of the world that Catholic schools were only for the rich?

When the Council began, other issues—such as liturgy, revelation, the nature of the church, ecumenism and so on—took center

Declaration on Christian Education

This document is not divided into chapters, but contains a preface, twelve articles and a conclusion.

stage. It was not until late in the third session that the bishops got around to debating education. By that point, the preparatory draft "On Catholic Schools" had been cut down in length twice, and then completely scrapped. A new text was prepared that affirmed Catholic schools within the wider context of Christian education. Because things were so different in different parts of the world, the new document did not get into specifics. Instead it only stated general themes. The text was approved in principle at the third session, further revised and formally promulgated at the fourth session (October 28, 1965).

READING GUIDE

The Preface of *GE* begins by noting the great importance of education *(gravissimum educationis)* in the world today. It explains that the church is interested in education because it is committed to promoting the total welfare of people: The church serves not just people's spiritual lives but their whole lives. An emphasis on a holistic approach to education runs throughout the document.

EDUCATION IN GENERAL (*GE*, 1–6)

Speaking not just of Christians and not just of religious training, the document states that all people have a right to education. Education serves the common good and ought to form people morally (*GE*, 1). Christians, in turn, have a right to a specifically Christian education (*GE*, 2). Parents, the state and the church all have a role to play in educating children (*GE*, 3).

Schools—of all kinds—are a crucial component in the education of children, and teachers deserve special recognition (*GE*, 5). The document affirms the right of parents to choose the school for their children. Thus the government should distribute public funds to various schools in such a way that parents are truly free to make this choice (*GE*, 6). This passage was something of a disappointment to many American bishops, including Cardinal Spellman of New York, who wanted the Council to explicitly state that the government has an obligation to support religious education. However, a more nuanced passage was thought to be necessary given the variety of ways governments relate to church-sponsored education.

CATHOLIC SCHOOLS (*GE*, 7–12)

Catholic children who do not go to Catholic schools were once viewed suspiciously by the church. But *GE* addresses them with sympathy and solidarity. The document calls on everyone to help with the religious education of these students (*GE*, 7). The text then moves to Catholic schools themselves. It unambiguously affirms their importance, asserts the right of the church to establish schools and reminds all Catholics of their duty to support them—including sending their children to Catholic schools wherever this is possible (*GE*, 8).

Colleges and universities contribute to the promotion of culture and the progress of society; they should enjoy a true liberty of exploration. Catholic universities ought to be promoted around the world (*GE*, 10). Their theology faculties contribute to the good of the church by training leaders and by deepening the whole church's appreciation of revelation (*GE*, 11). Cooperation among all these various educational enterprises is key (*GE*, 12). Finally, the document concludes with an exhortation thanking educators and encouraging students to consider becoming teachers.

THE DOCUMENT TODAY

RELIGIOUS EDUCATION AFTER THE COUNCIL

In 1971, the Vatican's Congregation for the Clergy issued a *General Catechetical Directory*. The *Directory* encouraged teachers to allow Christianity to take root in various cultures and situations by exploring new methods and modes of explanation. This coincided with a veritable revolution in the broader field of education. Traditional methods were being questioned and radically new approaches were being proposed.

....

Subsidiarity

"In accordance with the principle of subsidiarity, when the efforts of the parents and of other organizations are inadequate [civil society] should itself undertake the duty of education, with due consideration, however, for the wishes of the parents" (*GE*, 3).

"Subsidiarity" is a principle of modern Catholic social teaching first articulated by Pope Pius XI in 1931. Basically, the principle states that the best social institutions for responding to a particular task are those closest to the situation. Larger institutions should not usurp smaller institutions when these smaller institutions can adequately respond to the need. But when local institutions (for example, a city government) cannot adequately respond, larger institutions (such as the state or federal government) have an obligation to support them. *GE* applies this principle twice to the role of government in education (*GE*, 3 and 6).

....

A period of catechetical experimentation exploded in the church of the United States. Religious educators abandoned the route memorization of the *Baltimore Catechism* and taught the faith by appealing to Scripture, liturgy and personal experience. Inductive approaches replaced deductive ones. And religious education became increasingly parish-based (and not solely school-based), as lay ministers were hired to coordinate catechetical programs, youth ministry and adult education. On the one hand, these new approaches offered a helpful reminder that being Catholic involves more than learning a list of doctrines or avoiding a list of sins. Religious formation must get in touch with the whole life experience of Catholics. On the other hand, some accuse these methods of being so thin in content that they have left behind a generation of Catholics with no clear sense of their religious identity.

CATHOLIC IDENTITY OF CATHOLIC COLLEGES AND UNIVERSITIES

In 1990, Pope John Paul II issued a letter dedicated to Catholic higher education called *Ex Corde Ecclesiae* ("From the Heart of the Church"). The document called these colleges and universities to a high standard in helping the church to achieve its mission. At the urging of the Vatican, the U.S. bishops subsequently developed norms for implementing *Ex Corde Ecclesiae* in the United States. Among these norms is the requirement that Catholic theologians obtain a *mandatum* from their local bishop that declares that the theologian is in full communion with the church and he or she will present Catholic doctrine as the official teaching of the church.

> **"** True education aims to give people a formation which is directed towards their final end and the good of that society to which they belong and in which, as adults, they will have their share of duties to perform **"** (*GE*, 1).

At first the debate over the *mandatum* was polarizing. Some complained that it infringed upon academic freedom. Others saw it simply as "truth in advertising." But out of these debates emerged several helpful observations. First, many theologians pointed out that the *mandatum* is redundant. Theologians *already* have the responsibility to present Catholic doctrine as the official position of the church (and not some other doctrine as if it were the church's teaching). But this responsibility flows from the obligations of professional competence, not from a *mandatum*. Second, others have warned that the *mandatum* threatens to blur the line between theology and catechesis, each of which makes a different contribution to the life of the church—the latter more explanatory, the former more exploratory. Finally, theologians have argued that too much of the burden is placed on them. There are many other ways in which a college or university expresses (or fails to express) its Catholic identity. For example, how much does the Catholic intellectual tradition permeate other departments? Does Catholic social teaching enter into the business school? Does the church's respect for life guide the medical school or the biology department? How does the institution as a whole live out its mission in the larger community? How successful is the school in preparing students to work for a more just world?

....

Catholic Schools in the United States

The Catholic school system in the United States grew up as an attempt to pass on the faith within a culture perceived to be unsupportive, even hostile, to it. Rejecting what they saw as the distinctively Protestant bias of the public schools, American Catholics chose to build their own. The Third Plenary Council of Baltimore (1884) mandated that every parish open a school within two years. It set the ideal as "every Catholic child in a Catholic school." That ideal was never reached. But thanks to generations of working immigrants who supported these schools and thousands of sisters and nuns who staffed them, the Catholic parochial system became an educational institution second in size only to the public schools. They reached their peak in the years following World War II. But demographic shifts from city to suburb, the virtual disappearance of women religious, and a new emphasis on parish-based religious education, have combined to inaugurate a new era of self-definition and mission for Catholic schools.

....

FOR REFLECTION

- Read *GE,* 4: Describe your own religious education. Would you describe it as home-based, parish-based or school-based? Was the emphasis more on personal experience or church beliefs? What are the advantages and disadvantages of your religious education?
- Read *GE,* 10–11: What is the mission of a Catholic university? How does that mission relate to the students—both Catholic and non-Catholic? What is the role of a theologian?

15

DECLARATION ON RELIGIOUS LIBERTY
Dignitatis Humanae

The Declaration on Religious Liberty *(DH)* was the most bitterly contested document of Vatican II. It was controversial because it raised in a pointed way a question that ran beneath the surface of the whole Council: How much was the church willing to change?

BEYOND A DOUBLE STANDARD

The claim that every individual has a right to practice his or her religion freely hardly seems controversial to us. But it was for some of the bishops at Vatican II. Why? To put it bluntly, the bishops had difficulty endorsing religious liberty because, for much of its history, the Catholic church had condemned it.

Ever since the Roman Emperor Constantine granted Christianity official status in the empire (313 AD), the church has sought ways to use the state to promote the faith. In Christian Europe throughout the Middle Ages, this worked well. Church and state were closely aligned. But following the eighteenth-century Enlightenment—and the political revolutions it spawned—the church was put on the defensive. Its privileged position was called into question, and even violently challenged. Thus to protect its interests, the Vatican formed treaties with secular governments, which were designed to salvage the special treatment the church had enjoyed for so long.

Declaration on Religious Liberty

On the Right of the Person and
 Communities to Social and Civil
 Liberty in Religious Matters

Chapter One: The General
 Principle of Religious Freedom

Chapter Two: Religious Freedom
 in the Light of Revelation

A theological theory had grown up to justify this special treatment. Because Catholics possess the truth, they alone have the right to practice and proclaim the faith—whether they live in a Catholic country or not. Other Christian churches and other religions do not have this right, because they are false. And "error has no rights." The government of a Catholic nation could decide to tolerate the religious practice of non-Catholics, if this were necessary in order to keep the peace. But such tolerance was seen as an exception, and not a right that non-Catholics could claim.

Critics were quick to point out the double standard at work here: The church demanded rights and freedoms where it was in the minority, but denied the same rights to others where it was in the majority.

The American Jesuit John Courtney Murray (1904–1967) was an articulate critic of this double standard. And, during the 1950s, the Vatican silenced him for his views. But the arguments he presented gradually took hold. Of course error has no rights, Murray said, neither does truth. For "error" and "truth" are abstract principles, and abstract principles have no rights. Only human beings have rights. By shifting the debate to the nature and dignity of the human person, Murray opened up the possibility of a new approach.

BORN OUT OF ECUMENISM

DH began as chapter five of the Decree on Ecumenism. From very early on, Cardinal Augustine Bea's Secretariat for Christian Unity recognized that without a clear affirmation of the right of all Christians to practice their faith, no real ecumenical dialogue would be possible. But during the second session, chapter five (along with chapter four on the Jewish people) was bracketed off from debate.

The "Black Week" of Vatican II

A string of events during the final week of the third session (November 14–21, 1964) left a cloud hanging over the bishops as they returned home to their dioceses. These events included (1) the presentation of the "Preliminary Note of Explanation," which qualified *LG*'s teaching on collegiality, (2) the postponement of the vote on religious liberty, (3) the addition of nineteen last-minute changes to the Decree on Ecumenism, and (4) the pope's declaration of Mary as "Mother of the Church," a title the Doctrinal Commission had consistently refused to include in *LG* for ecumenical and theological reasons. The cumulative effect of these developments left the council participants with a sense of suspicion and frustration with Pope Paul VI, who seemed to be imposing his will on the Council—without discussion or debate—in ways clearly favorable to that vocal minority of bishops opposed to church renewal. It is unfortunate that this dark mood marred the milestones achieved that same week: the promulgation of the Dogmatic Constitution on the Church, the Decree on Ecumenism, and the Decree on the Eastern Churches.

Most bishops wanted to endorse the principle of religious liberty. Thus they suspected that a small opposition was trying to keep the issue off the agenda. These opponents came mainly from Italy and Spain, where earlier treaties gave the church a range of state-protected privileges. These bishops believed that if the Council endorsed religious freedom, these privileges would be removed, and the faith would suffer. But even more troublesome for them was the issue of doctrinal development. In the face of what seemed to be unequivocal condemnations of religious liberty by past popes, how could the Council now approve this principle? The French Archbishop Marcel Lefebvre captured their concern and consternation when he said: "If what is being taught is true, then what the church has taught is false." To admit that church teaching changed would imply that the church had been wrong. This was too much for some bishops.

The Turbulent Third Session

Between the second and third sessions, the Coordinating Commission decided that religious liberty should stand on its own as an independent document. The text was debated in September 1964. But controversy continued over who was responsible for revisions. A crisis erupted in October when opponents of the document tried to turn it over to a mixed commission stacked with members who had openly criticized it. Quick action by Bea and a group of other cardinals kept the document under his jurisdiction. Still, a minority of powerful bishops seemed intent on killing the document.

A vote on religious liberty was then scheduled for the next-to-the-last day of the Council's third session (Thursday, November 19, 1964). But when that Thursday arrived, Cardinal Eugene Tisserant, dean of the council presidents, made a surprise announcement: Because there was not enough time to study the newly revised text, there would be no vote. The assembly erupted in protest and confusion. Apparently, the opposition had convinced the council leadership to postpone the vote. As Bishop De Smedt delivered his summary of the document, he was interrupted several times by loud and sustained applause—an effort by the majority to show their approval for the text. A petition was drafted on the spot, asking Pope Paul VI "urgently, very urgently, most urgently" *(instanter, instantius, instantissime)* to allow the vote to take place. Many feared that the delay would mean the demise of the document. In the end, the pope stood behind Tisserant's decision. But he promised that religious liberty would be the first item on the agenda when the Council reconvened the following fall.

The disappointment and discouragement over this delay was real. But, in hindsight, it may have been for the best. Even John Courtney Murray (who at that point was deeply involved in the drafting of the text) admitted that postponing the vote actually helped the document. Further revisions led to a stronger text, a text finally promulgated on December 7, 1965.

READING GUIDE

DH begins with the recognition that people today have become increasingly aware of the dignity of the human person *(dignitatis humanae),* a dignity that demands the freedom to act according to one's religious convictions. The introductory article then addresses two contentious issues. First, the affirmation of the right to religious freedom does not imply that all religions are the same. The text states that the teachings of the Catholic church are true. But it recognizes that truth cannot be forced. People must be allowed the freedom to accept or reject truth for themselves. Second, the text makes clear the Council's intention to develop the teaching of recent popes. It admits that, on this issue, church teaching has changed.

> **"** Truth can impose itself on the human mind by the force of its own truth, which wins over the mind with both gentleness and power **"** (*DH*, 1).

In endorsing religious freedom, the two chapters that follow present arguments based on reason (chapter one) and revelation (chapter two).

CHAPTER ONE: THE GENERAL PRINCIPLE OF RELIGIOUS FREEDOM (*DH*, 2–8)

The Human Person (*DH*, 2–3)

Religious freedom is not merely to be tolerated, as it was in past papal statements. Religious freedom is to be affirmed as a right. This right is based on the dignity of the human person, who is endowed by God with reason and free will. The nature of the search for truth demands free inquiry. And no one should be forced to act against her or his conscience. This personal right to religious freedom must be granted constitutional recognition by governments as a true civil right.

Religious Communities (*DH*, 4–8)

Human beings are social by nature. They must be allowed to give external expression to their internal beliefs about God. Therefore, religious liberty must extend beyond individuals to religious communities

An American Issue

The American hierarchy adopted religious liberty as their issue, the distinctive contribution American Catholicism could make to the Second Vatican Council. Here they found a cause for renewal that would not scandalize the faithful back home. The early intervention of Cardinal Francis Spellman of New York was decisive in keeping religious liberty on the agenda. (Spellman was also responsible for getting John Courtney Murray—formerly silenced by Rome—appointed as a council expert.) And the American bishops together coordinated a united front in support of the declaration.

themselves. All religious groups should have the right to appoint their ministers, buy property, build buildings, teach publicly, communicate freely and engage in all those activities that constitute the exercise of their religion—insofar as these activities do not infringe on the rights of others (*DH,* 4). Every family has the right to worship as it chooses, and parents have the right to provide for the religious education of their children (*DH,* 5). After listing the duties and limits of government (*DH,* 6–7), chapter one ends with an exhortation for the responsible use of freedom (*DH,* 8).

CHAPTER TWO: RELIGIOUS FREEDOM IN THE LIGHT OF REVELATION (*DH,* 9–15)

Chapter two claims that religious liberty is rooted in revelation—not because the Bible speaks directly about it, but because the Bible reveals to us more fully the dignity of the human person on which religious liberty rests. Jesus provides the example. He did not force people to follow him, nor did he coerce participation. Instead he acted patiently. He offered an invitation, but left his listeners free to respond on their own (*DH,* 11). The apostles followed this example. And the church, despite a sad history of actions to the contrary, has nevertheless affirmed in its official teaching that no one can be coerced into believing (*DH,* 12). The document ends by returning to the contemporary situation, praising those movements toward religious liberty among nations and denouncing those that have sought to curtail the free exercise of religion.

THE DOCUMENT TODAY

DEVELOPMENT OF DOCTRINE

Shortly after the Council ended, John Courtney Murray wrote that the issue of doctrinal development was *the* issue running beneath the surface of all the Council's debates. *DH* formally acknowledges development in the church's teaching on religious liberty. But it never explains how doctrinal development itself is to be understood. How can the church, which claims to teach the truth, change its teaching? In his opening speech to the Council, John XXIII distinguished between the substance of the ancient doctrine and the way in which it is presented. But can we so easily separate these two? And aren't there genuine changes not only in presentation, but also in substance (the teaching on religious liberty, for example, or the church's past condemnations of lending money at interest)?

Some theologians have argued that later doctrinal statements are simply the logical development of insights contained in the Bible. Others point to the deeper meaning of revelation as spelled out in the Council's Constitution on Divine Revelation *(DV).* If revelation itself is not primarily words *about* God, but a living encounter *with* God, then we can admit that our limited human words often fail to capture this mystery. In such a view, doctrinal development is our becoming more and more conscious of all that is contained in God's offer of friendship. What is present implicitly from the beginning gradually becomes explicit in the church as we grow in our relationship with God.

THE MEANING OF FREEDOM

In the United States especially, "freedom" is a value constantly celebrated but rarely defined. What does "freedom" mean? *DH* presents

Post-Conciliar Schism

The only significant schism to occur as a result of Vatican II was that of the followers of the French Archbishop Marcel Lefebvre (1905–1991). Lefebvre attended Vatican II, but disagreed with much of its agenda for renewal, refusing to sign some of the final documents. Among his complaints were the reform of the liturgy, the council's openness to non-Christian religions, and, especially, its teaching on religious liberty. "Lefebvrites" believe that Vatican II formally entered into heresy with the Declaration on Religious Liberty. In 1988, after ordaining four bishops without papal authorization, Lefebvre was formally excommunicated. Today, the Society of Saint Pius X, the heirs to Lefebvre's schism, includes about two hundred thousand members worldwide.

freedom primarily as protection against coercion or interference by the state in religious matters. And we tend to assume this negative definition in our political rhetoric: Freedom means freedom from tyranny, freedom from interference, freedom from constraints so that I can do what *I* want to do. But freedom need not be so narrowly understood. *DH,* 8 encourages the responsible use of freedom; it sees true freedom in people who are oriented toward what is true and just. And popes since the Council—particularly Pope Benedict XVI—have invited Catholics to think of freedom not simply as freedom *from* coercion, but as freedom *for* the good. Freedom, Pope Benedict proclaims, is not about doing what *I* want, but doing what *God* wants. For in this is truth, the truth that sets one free.

FREEDOM WITHIN THE CHURCH

DH took up the question of religious liberty in the context of the relationship between church and state. It did not seek to address the issue of religious liberty *within* the church. Yet many of the debates that have emerged since the Council revolve around just this question. How free are Catholics to voice their concerns to the hierarchy? How free are they to live out their convictions when their convictions do not conform to church teaching? How free are they to practice their faith in ways meaningful to them? Some might argue that internal freedom has vastly expanded (on issues like birth control or Mass attendance, Catholics seem to feel free to do what they choose). Others might argue that freedom has been curtailed (take, for example, the censoring of theologians or the limitations placed on liturgical adaptation). And many debate whether these developments have been healthy or harmful.

FOR REFLECTION

• Read *DH,* 1: What are the implications of admitting change in the church and in church teaching? How would you distinguish between what is changeable and what is not? How would you distinguish legitimate development from illegitimate development?

• Read *DH,* 8: Reflect on your own assumptions about freedom. What does it mean to you? How do you see the language of freedom used in our society today? Does the idea that following God is "freeing" speak to you?

• Read *DH,* 9–11: Is there too much freedom in the church today or too little? Name one area where you feel too much freedom has been allowed. Name one area of church life where there is not enough freedom. Does the distinction between freedom *from* and freedom *for* help here?

DECLARATION ON THE RELATION OF THE CHURCH TO NON-CHRISTIAN RELIGIONS
Nostra Aetate

What role the great religions of the world play in God's saving plan is one of the most challenging questions facing the church today. But in preparing for Vatican II, the issue hardly came up. No one planned anything like the Declaration on the Relation of the Church to Non-Christian Religions *(NA)*. Instead, Pope John XXIII simply wanted a statement on the Jews, one that would address the evils of anti-Semitism. But the effort to produce a statement on Judaism led— almost by chance—to a short text on all religions. This "providential afterthought" turned out to be one of the great achievements of the Second Vatican Council.

THE CHURCH AND THE JEWISH PEOPLE

The tragedy of the Holocaust *(Shoah)* forced the church to face its own sad history of condemnation, prejudice and persecution directed toward Jews. Pope John saw this. He knew that the Council could not afford to be silent on this issue. And so he personally entrusted Cardinal Bea with the task of preparing a statement on proper Christian attitudes toward Jews.

In the months leading up to Vatican II, Cardinal Bea's Secretariat for Christian Unity produced a brief statement that challenged past assumptions Catholics have made about Judaism. To those who had forgotten Christianity's Jewish roots, the draft recovered the ancient links between the church and Israel. To those who thought that God had rejected the Jews, the text repeated Saint Paul's claim that the Jewish people remain dear to God. And to those who still harbored irrational suspicions and prejudice, the document condemned anti-Semitism in all its forms.

....

Declaration on the Relation of the Church to Non-Christian Religions

The document is not divided into chapters but contains five articles.

....

The summer before the Council began, in June of 1962, the Central Preparatory Commission rejected Cardinal Bea's text. The reason was not theological but political. Bishops from Arab countries opposed the document for fear that a positive statement on the Jews would be interpreted as an endorsement of the state of Israel. Christians in Arab nations were afraid that they might suffer reprisals as a result. Their fears were not unfounded. Arab governments had already begun to apply pressure on the Vatican Secretariat of State through diplomatic channels. They complained that the church was taking sides in the political dispute between the Israelis and the Palestinians.

Cardinal Bea did not give up. Between the Council's first and second sessions, he rescued the statement on the Jews by including it as chapter four in the Decree on Ecumenism. This chapter was submitted to the bishops for consideration, but not debated. Along with chapter five on religious liberty, chapter four was separated from the ecumenism decree, and time ran out before it could be discussed. In his closing remarks at the end of the second session, Cardinal Bea assured the assembly that "What is put off is not put away."

THE MUSTARD SEED BECOMES A TREE
By this point, the "Decree on the Jews" had aroused interest worldwide. So when reports spread in the spring of 1964 that the text was being watered down, Jewish leaders and concerned Catholics

❝ We cannot truly pray to God the Father of all if we treat any people as other than sisters and brothers, for all are created in God's image **❞** (NA, 5).

protested. In April, the Council's Coordinating Commission had eliminated a few passages and made several other changes that, all in all, gave the text a "less friendly" tone. Moreover, in order to satisfy objections coming from the Arab world, the commission asked that the document treat not just Jews, but Muslims as well.

Thus the text that the bishops debated at the beginning of the third session was much weaker than the original. And it was criticized on this account. Most of those who spoke asked for a stronger and more positive statement about Judaism. They wanted put back in what had been taken out. A few bishops maintained their opposition to the draft as a whole. The Arab bishops, still convinced that it unfairly promoted Jewish religious and political concerns, asked that the document be withdrawn.

Instead, Cardinal Bea's secretariat chose to expand the document in a way that radically broadened its perspective. Rather than allow its text to remain eviscerated—or dropped entirely—the secretariat placed its treatment of the Jewish people within the context of a serious consideration of the other great religions of the world. The Decree on the Jews became the Declaration on the Relation of the Church to Non-Christian Religions. Reflecting later on the troubled history of this declaration, John Oesterreicher (one of the architects of the document) observed that the opposition faced by this text had a positive result: It forced the Council to consider entirely new horizons. In presenting the expanded document to the assembly, Cardinal Bea pointed to a parable. What began as a small mustard seed—a brief statement on the right attitude of Christians to the Jewish people—had grown to become a tree in which all religions could build their nests. The declaration was approved and formally promulgated on October 28, 1965.

....

The Church Deplores Anti-Semitism

"Remembering, then, its common heritage with the Jews and moved not by any political consideration, but solely by the religious motivation of christian charity, [the church] deplores all hatreds, persecutions, displays of anti-semitism levelled at any time or from any source against the Jews" (NA, 4).

The Latin phrase for "and condemns" was cut from an earlier version of this sentence (leaving the weaker verb "deplores")—leading some commentators to accuse the Council of softening its rejection of anti-Semitism. Several bishops requested the change to avoid giving the impression that the Council was repudiating discrimination against Jews more forcefully than discrimination against other groups. Others argued that John XXIII had asked this pastoral Council to avoid condemnations altogether.

....

READING GUIDE

NA opens with an optimism that carries through the entire document: In our times *(nostra aetate),* people are coming together and the bonds of friendship are growing stronger. We should begin with what we have in common, the introduction states, for humanity forms one community with the same divine source and goal (NA, 1).

RELIGIONS OF THE WORLD (NA, 2–3)

The document's method is simple. Rather than highlight differences or attempt to resolve theological disputes, NA first points out a few specific commonalities and then invites dialogue. It offers brief, but positive, descriptions of the great religious traditions of the world: Hinduism is expressed in profound myth and penetrating philosophy, it encourages asceticism, meditation and the love of God. Buddhism acknowledges the inadequacy of this changing world. Muslims worship the one God; they link their faith to Abraham and honor Jesus as a prophet; they praise his virgin mother. Such remarks are far from a comprehensive introduction. Instead they provide a starting point for future discussion and collaboration.

Beneath these warm words is a substantive claim: "The Catholic Church rejects nothing of what is true and holy in these religions." While *NA* affirms the church's mission to proclaim Christ without fail, it acknowledges that other religions often "reflect a ray of that truth which enlightens all men and women" (*NA,* 2).

JUDAISM (*NA*, 4)

After reflecting on the deep spiritual links between Israel and the church, *NA* affirms that the Jewish people remain very dear to God. The text repeats Saint Paul's claim about the covenant with Israel: "God does not take back the gifts he bestowed or the choice he made" (*NA,* 4; see also Romans 11:28–29). The sentence that follows speaks with hope of the day when all people will serve God shoulder to shoulder. An earlier draft spoke of the "conversion" of Jews. However, this language was seen as inappropriate and dropped. Instead of wishing for Jews to convert, the text points to the future reign of God in which all people will be one.

During the drafting and discussion of *NA,* intense debate surrounded the word *deicide* ("killing God"). Due to the role some Jewish leaders played in the death of Jesus, Christians over the centuries had come to accuse the Jews of this crime. If the Jews had sought to kill God, God in turn must have rejected the Jews. Such was a common Christian view throughout the Middle Ages and into the modern era. To repudiate this view, early drafts of *NA* explicitly stated that the Jews are not guilty of deicide. But to the dismay of many bishops, the word *deicide* dropped out in subsequent revisions (due to political pressure from the Arab world and theological ambiguities with the word itself). However, the substance of the earlier text remained: Neither all Jews then, nor any Jew today, can be blamed for the death of Jesus. Jews should not be described as rejected or cursed by God. Finally, the text makes a clear statement that the church deplores all hatred, persecution and anti-Semitism.

DISCRIMINATION (*NA*, 5)

A concluding article places the Council's comments on anti-Semitism within a broader rejection of all forms of discrimination, whether based on race, color, condition in life or religion. All people are created in God's image. We cannot pray to God as Father if we do not treat all people as our sisters and brothers.

THE DOCUMENT TODAY

SUPERSESSIONISM

The discrimination of Jews that *NA* so forcefully rejects has, over the centuries, taken theological shape as "supersessionism"—the claim that Christianity has totally superseded Judaism and thus made Judaism no longer significant in the history of salvation. This tendency to ignore the Jewish roots of Christianity, to reduce the Hebrew Bible to a collection of prophecies pointing toward Christ, to see the New Testament rendering void the covenant with Israel, to imagine Judaism as a historical curiosity rather than a living religion—these have shaped centuries of anti-Semitism. But supersessionism ignores Saint Paul's basic claim (repeated by *NA*) that God keeps his promises, and that the Jews remain dear to the God who called Abraham.

SALVATION AND OTHER RELIGIONS

Vatican II clearly affirmed the possibility of salvation for those outside of the church (see *LG,* 16; *GS,* 22). Since then, theologians have focused not so much on the salvation of individuals in other religions, but on the saving value of the religions themselves. What role, if any, do these other religions play in the salvation of their members? Are non-Christians saved *despite* their own religious beliefs and practices or *because* of them? *NA* spoke very positively about these other religions. But do these religions save their members? It left this question open.

At least three positions can be identified in recent theological debates on this issue:

The Good Friday Liturgy

Well into the twentieth century, every Holy Week Catholics prayed for "the perfidious Jews." The prayer came in the middle of the solemn intercessions on Good Friday. Pope Pius XII quietly dropped the adjective "perfidious" in his own prayer. And in 1959 John XXIII ordered that this offensive language be removed from the official liturgy of the church.

The *exclusivist* position interprets Christ's words literally, "No one comes to the Father except through me" (John 14:6). Salvation is granted in and through the church alone. Other religions are false and misleading. This viewpoint was held by many Catholics up until Vatican II, but it was clearly set aside by the Council.

The *inclusivist* position takes Christ's words seriously, but recognizes that Christ may work through other religions in a hidden way. Proponents of this view argue that when people of any religion strive to live a moral life, trying to do the will of God or to follow their conscience, they are in fact being guided by Christ. These people are saying yes to Christ, even if they do not know it. This position tries to balance the belief that Christ is the one unique savior of the world alongside the possibility of salvation for the good Buddhist or Muslim (for example). It is the position closest to the church's official teaching today.

The *pluralist* position argues that Christ is an important savior, but not the only one. Figures in other religions (such as Buddha or Krishna) also offer salvation for their members, often revealing values that Christians overlook.

Another approach avoids the issue of salvation altogether, emphasizing instead the need for *dialogue* and mutual understanding. The hope here is that dialogue will lead to new ways of considering the question that have not yet been considered.

A WORLD-CHURCH

Shortly after Vatican II, the German theologian Karl Rahner wrote a short essay that remains one of the most important interpretations of the Council. His basic thesis stated that, as a result of Vatican II, the church became for the first time a truly *world-church*. Rahner divided all of Christian history into three periods: (1) the period of Jewish-Christianity, relatively brief, in which followers of Jesus remained entirely within the context of Judaism; (2) the period of European Christianity, which began with the acceptance of Gentiles into the church in the first century and extended up into the twentieth century, and (3) the period of the world-church, only just begun. It is true that the church existed around the world prior to the twentieth century. But it existed, as Rahner put it, as a kind of "export firm," exporting *European* Christianity (which had as much to do with culture as with religion) to the rest of the world. Vatican II opened the door to a truly world-church, one that doesn't simply export a finished product, but one that openly engages other peoples, cultures and mentalities. The change from the Latin Mass to the vernacular is a clear symbol of this change—a change Rahner also saw in the Council's attention to the collegiality of bishops, its new vision of missionary activity, and its openness to other religions.

FOR REFLECTION

• Read *NA,* 4: Can you name examples of supersessionism from your own experience? How do you suggest speaking of Christ in ways that avoid dismissing God's covenant with Israel?

• Read *NA,* 2–3: What other passages from the documents of Vatican II shed light on the salvation of non-Christians? What are the advantages and disadvantages of the exclusivist, inclusivist and pluralist positions? Where do you locate yourself along this spectrum?

• Read *NA,* 1: Do you agree with Rahner's interpretation? Has the church become a world-church? What developments have fostered a more global vision of the church? What developments have impeded this vision? What does the future of the church hold?

GLOSSARY

....

aggiornamento: Italian for "bringing up to date," used by Pope John XXIII to describe his hopes for church renewal at Vatican II.

apostolate: the participation in the mission of the church.

Apostolic See: refers to the pope and those agencies within the Roman Curia that help the pope in his governance of the universal church; also called the "Holy See."

apostolic succession: the handing on of the mission of the apostles to those who followed them, the bishops. This direct historical continuity between the apostles and church leaders today is one of the requirements the Catholic church maintains is necessary for valid ordained ministry.

bishops' conference: *See* episcopal conference.

cardinal: title given to those high-ranking church officials (usually the leaders of important archdioceses or Vatican offices) who elect the pope and serve as his closest advisers.

catechumen: one who is formally preparing for baptism into the church.

Catholic Eastern Churches: Christian churches that follow one of several Eastern liturgical rites and that exist in full union with Rome. While maintaining communion with the pope, these churches retain their own liturgies, church law, structures of government and traditions.

Catholic social teaching: a body of teaching material—including Vatican II's Pastoral Constitution on the Church in the Modern World—that treats the political, social and economic implications of the gospel.

charism: spiritual gifts given by the Holy Spirit to individuals or groups for the good of the community; charism of an individual can become embodied in a larger group, such as a religious order, allowing the charism to carry on (for example, Saint Francis embraced poverty for the sake of Christ; this charism became embodied in the Franciscan order, whose members continue to embrace poverty in order to serve God and others).

collegiality: the sharing of authority among bishops and the pope.

commissions: name given to the various committees of the Second Vatican Council; these included the preparatory commissions (which drafted documents before the Council began) and the conciliar commissions (which worked on the documents while the Council was in session). A central coordinating commission oversaw the work of the various commissions.

concelebration: the participation of more than one ordained priest in the same liturgical celebration.

constitution: Vatican II issued four of these documents (*SC, DV, LG* and *GS*), which treat substantive doctrinal issues that pertain to the very nature of the church—the most solemn and formal type of document issued by an ecumenical council.

council: official gathering of bishops and other church leaders called together to discuss and make decisions on matters pertaining to the church; an ecumenical council is a "worldwide" gathering of bishops that represents the highest level of their teaching authority.

curia: the various governing agencies that support bishops in their ministry; the term usually refers to the Roman Curia, those offices and officials who assist the pope in his administration of the universal church.

declaration: Vatican II issued three of these documents (*GE, DH* and *NA*), which take up particular issues of contemporary interest or pastoral concern.

decree: Vatican II issued nine of these documents (*CD, PO, OT, PC, AA, UR, OE, IM* and *AG*), which draw on the doctrinal principles articulated in the constitutions and apply them to specific issues or groups within the church.

diaconate: the order of deacons; Vatican II reinstated the diaconate as a permanent order within the church (alongside bishops and priests) and opened it to married men.

ecclesiology: the study of the nature and mission of the church.

ecumenism: meaning "the whole world," the term refers to those efforts that seek to reunify the separated Christian churches.

encyclical: a formal letter, written by the pope and addressed to the whole church, that treats moral, theological or practical issues.

episcopal conference: a national or regional gathering of bishops established in order to address common issues facing the church in their area.

episcopate: the order of bishops.

eschatology: the study of the "last things"—heaven, hell, judgment and the coming reign of God.

evangelical counsels: the ideals of poverty, chastity and obedience, which are embraced through public vows by those in religious life.

heresy: the rejection of a belief that is part of church dogma.

hierarchy: includes all the clergy (bishops, priests, deacons), but usually refers to the bishops alone.

Holy Office: the Vatican office responsible for questions of doctrine, led by Cardinal Alfredo Ottaviani at the time of Vatican II and now titled the Congregation for the Doctrine of the Faith.

inerrancy: the belief that the Bible is without error insofar as it teaches truth for our salvation; according to Vatican II, inerrancy does not necessarily imply that the Bible is always historically or scientifically accurate.

inspiration: the belief that the Bible is the Word of God in human words.

intercommunion: the sharing in liturgical worship, especially the Eucharist, between separated Christians.

just war: refers to an approach that argues that war is morally justifiable in certain circumstances and under certain conditions (these conditions include having a just cause, entering with the right intention, declaring war as a last resort and so on).

laity: the Christian faithful who are not ordained and who do not belong to a community of religious life.

liturgy: the public and official worship of the church; usually refers to the Mass, but includes other public prayer as well.

observers: non-voting attendees of the Second Vatican Council. Vatican II was the first ecumenical council to include non-Catholics and women as official observers. While they did not vote, they played an active role in the work of several conciliar commissions.

particular church: refers primarily to a diocese headed by a bishop.

pastoral: an adjective that evokes the image of a good shepherd caring for his sheep, often used to describe the church's ministry of preaching, prayer and service to those in need. By calling Vatican II a "pastoral" council, John XXIII signaled that it would focus not primarily on abstract doctrine, but on the concrete needs of the church and the world, offering to serve in imitation of Christ the Good Shepherd.

patriarch: a bishop who presides over an autonomous federation of dioceses, called a patriarchate.

Pentecost: the descent of the Holy Spirit on the apostles fifty days after Easter (see Acts 2:1–41). Pope John XXIII called Vatican II a "new Pentecost" because he believed the Spirit was working through it to inspire the church to recover the zeal of the first apostles.

pontiff: literally, "bridge-builder," another name for the pope.

primacy, papal: the authority possessed by the pope, by virtue of his office, to act as head of the universal church; distinct from papal infallibility, which refers to the pope's capacity to define essential teachings as certainly true.

reception: the process by which a teaching or decision of the church is accepted (or not accepted) by the Christian faithful; reception is not necessary to legitimate or validate the truth taught, but it does indicate whether the teaching is effective and relevant within the life of the community.

religious life: a way of living the Christian faith that involves committing to a particular community (such as the Benedictines or the Dominicans) and professing the vows of poverty, chastity and obedience. Those in religious life are commonly called sisters, nuns, brothers or monks (religious order priests are also included).

ressourcement: French for "return to the sources," used to describe the work of Catholic Scripture scholars, theologians and experts in liturgy who helped prepare for Vatican II by recovering the great "classics" of the Christian tradition.

revelation: the disclosure of God's very self to humanity, a disclosure mediated to us in a unique way by the testimony of Scripture.

rite: refers either to a particular liturgical ceremony (such as the rite of baptism) or to a distinct liturgical "family," in which all of the individual ceremonies together form a recognizable and recognized tradition (such as the Roman rite or the Byzantine rite).

schema: Latin word referring to the draft documents that were debated at Vatican II.

schism: a formal split between churches or groups of Christians.

secretariat: title given to some of the committees that assisted with preparations for the Second Vatican Council, the most influential of which was the Secretariat for Promoting Christian Unity led by Cardinal Augustine Bea. After the Council, some secretariats became permanent offices in the Roman Curia.

sense of the faith/sense of the faithful: both terms (in Latin, *sensus fidei* and *sensus fidelium*) point to the church's belief that the whole body of believers is granted by God an intuitive sense of what is true; official church teaching emerges out of the experience of the whole church and ought to resonate with it.

subsidiarity: a principle of Catholic social teaching which states that the best institutions for responding to a particular task are those closest to the situation.

synod: like a council, an official gathering of church leaders, but usually more limited in scope. At Vatican II, Pope Paul VI established a worldwide synod of bishops, in which representatives would meet periodically to advise the pope on important matters.

threefold work of Christ: the traditional designation of Christ as prophet, priest and king became a major organizational principle in the Vatican II documents, used to describe the ways in which a variety of groups within the church teach, sanctify and serve.

vernacular: the native language of a particular people or region.

FOR FURTHER READING

....

The Documents of Vatican II

www.vatican.va. All of the documents—in several languages—are available on the Vatican's official Web site.

Vatican Council II: The Basic Sixteen Documents, edited by Austin Flannery, O.P. (Northport, N.Y.: Costello, 1996). A revised translation in gender-inclusive language. This is the version used throughout this book.

The Documents of Vatican II, edited by Walter M. Abbott, S.J. (New York: Guild, 1966). The first mass-market English translation to appear in the United States.

Decrees of the Ecumenical Councils, two volumes, edited by Norman P. Tanner, S.J. (London: Sheed & Ward/Washington, D.C.: Georgetown University Press, 1990). English translations of the documents of the twenty-one general councils, from Nicaea to Vatican II, along with original Greek or Latin.

Major Reference Works

Acta Synodalia Sacrosancti Concilii Oecumenici Vaticani II, four volumes (Vatican City: Typis Polyglottis Vaticanis, 1970–1980). The official minutes of Vatican II, containing the Latin text of the Council's procedures, decisions, speeches and final texts. Its four "volumes" are in fact twenty-five massive tomes of over eight hundred pages each. Another twenty-three volumes document the preparation for the Council.

Council Daybook, three volumes, edited by Floyd Anderson (Washington, D.C.: National Catholic Welfare Conference, 1965–1966). A collection of press releases that summarize the activities and debates for every day that the Council was in session; also includes important papal speeches, the final council documents and an extensive index.

History of Vatican II, five volumes, edited by Giuseppe Alberigo and Joseph A. Komonchak (Maryknoll, N.Y.: Orbis, 1995–2005). The definitive history of the Council.

Commentary on the Documents of Vatican II, five volumes, edited by Herbert Vorgrimler (New York: Herder and Herder, 1967–1969). The standard commentary prepared by a team of European scholars, many of whom served as theological experts at Vatican II.

Rediscovering Vatican II, eight volumes, edited by Christopher Bellitto (New York: Paulist, 2005—). This series treats all sixteen documents in their historical context, central themes and subsequent reception by the church. Titles include *Ecumenism and Interreligious Dialogue,* by Edward Idris Cardinal Cassidy, and *The Church and the World,* by Norman Tanner, with others to come.

Vatican II: Assessment and Perspectives Twenty-Five Years After (1962–1987), three volumes, edited by René Latourelle (New York: Paulist, 1989). A collection of scholarly articles on the Council and its implementation.

Vatican Council II: The Conciliar and Post-Conciliar Documents and *Vatican Council II: More Post-Conciliar Documents,* edited by Austin Flannery, o.p. (Northport, N.Y.: Costello, 1996, 1998). This two-volume set includes the sixteen Vatican II documents along with important church documents issued after the Council.

Vatican Council II, by Xavier Rynne (Francis X. Murphy) (Maryknoll, N.Y.: Orbis, 1999). A reprint of Murphy's famous "Letters from Vatican City," which originally appeared in *The New Yorker.* These letters summarize the council debates in a lively way, pointing out the personalities and political maneuvering behind Vatican II.

Other Useful Resources

Doyle, Dennis M., *The Church Emerging from Vatican II: A Popular Approach to Contemporary Catholicism*, revised edition (Mystic, Conn.: Twenty-Third, 2006).

Hastings, Adrian, ed., *Modern Catholicism: Vatican II and After* (New York: Oxford University Press, 1990).

Huebsch, Bill, *Vatican II in Plain English*, three volumes (Allen, Tex.: Thomas More, 1997).

Madges, William and Michael J. Daley, eds., *Vatican II: Forty Personal Stories* (Mystic, Conn.: Twenty-Third, 2003).

McBrien, Richard P., *Catholicism* (San Francisco: HarperSanFrancisco, 1994).

Miller, John H., c.s.c., ed., *Vatican II: An Interfaith Appraisal* (Notre Dame, Ind.: University of Notre Dame Press, 1966).

O'Connell, Timothy E., ed., *Vatican II and Its Documents: An American Reappraisal* (Wilmington, Del.: Michael Glazier, 1986).

Rush, Ormond, *Still Interpreting Vatican II: Some Hermeneutical Principles* (New York: Paulist, 2004).

Stacpoole, Alberic, ed., *Vatican II Revisited: By Those Who Were There* (Minneapolis: Winston, 1986).

Sullivan, Maureen, o.p., *101 Questions and Answers on Vatican II* (New York: Paulist, 2002).

INDEX

....